The Psychology of Religion

The Psychology of Religion

AN INTRODUCTION

L. B. Brown

First published in Great Britain 1988
SPCK
Holy Trinity Church
Marylebone Road
London NW1 4DU

ACKNOWLEDGEMENTS
Thanks are due to the following for permission
to reproduce copyright material:

Faber and Faber Ltd for the extract from
Waiting for Godot by Samuel Beckett.
Pink Floyd Music Publishers Ltd for the
extract from 'The final cut'.

British Library Cataloguing in Publication Data

Brown, L. B.
   The psychology of religion: an introduction.
   1. Psychology, Religious
   I. Title
   200'.1'9   BL53
   ISBN 0-281-04335-3

Typeset by Rowland Phototypesetting Ltd
Bury St Edmunds, Suffolk
Printed in Great Britain by
Hollen Street Press Ltd, Slough, Berks

Contents

Contents

Introduction

This is a book for those interested in the study of religion, however that is defined. It shows how contemporary psychology has approached religion, and I hope it will prove as useful for those with some knowledge of psychology who want to know how it deals with religious questions as for those primarily concerned with the study of theology and religion who wonder about psychological approaches to their subject.

The early nineteenth-century psychologists turned to religion as a natural area of study, since their interest in psychology had emerged from theology as much as from philosophy and physiology. By the beginning of the twentieth century, psychologists were greatly concerned with relationships between body, mind and society. Today, psychology can be described in terms of exploring behaviour, beliefs and experience in aesthetic, moral, pragmatic, religious and other contexts. It recognizes that our actions and beliefs may be functional or dysfunctional, and under personal, social or institutional control.

Although the early interest in the psychology of religion declined during the 1930s, when psychology rather single-mindedly pursued the study of behaviour as if little else was of any interest, that bias began to change in the 1950s. Behaviourism fell out of favour then because it had neglected the role of deliberate awareness and the cognitive processes underlying human action. Helped by the work of Gordon Allport in the United States and Robert Thouless in Britain and under the umbrella of 'the scientific study of religion' the psychology of religion revived during the 1960s.

My approach aims to apply academic psychology to some of the issues that religion presents to us, showing how psychological methods and theories have been used to interpret or understand religious belief and practice. The validity of the findings from psychological studies of religion is established by their consistency and coherence. Psychologists usually talk about the way particular religious beliefs influence behaviour, leaving questions about the *truth* of those beliefs to philosophy and theology. Their findings are sometimes used by both believers and unbelievers to support their own beliefs, but the once fashionable application of psychological theories to resolve theological or existential problems has been replaced by the use of psychological methods and findings to evaluate the work of religion and of other branches of the 'caring professions'.

Whether psychological research can ever be decentered and value-free is not readily settled, since it is almost impossible for any scientist to be completely detached from his or her own interests or prejudices. Mine derive from a religious background in Methodism and the Church of England, training in general psychology, and work in medical and social settings as well as in the psychology of religion (Brown, 1973, 1985, 1987). I am indebted to James Embury and William Binet Brown, who were steeped in Protestantism and who have been influences since my childhood. (I am also grateful to Louise Kahabka for so capably typing the several drafts of this manuscript.)

Despite the extensive literature in the psychology of religion, which is almost entirely concerned with Christianity (cf. Capps, Rambo and Ransohoff, 1976; Van de Kemp and Malony, 1984), I have tried not to give too many references. Empirical support *is* available for all my statements, though of course others might interpret the evidence differently. Furthermore, every science reflects an evolving consensus, and is continually testing, refining and discarding its theories in the light of fresh evidence.

The dominant areas of interest among psychologists of religion have moved from describing the experiences of religious people to a current preoccupation with the measurement of religious beliefs and attitudes in order to compare groups or identify the deeper structures that support religion (Gorsuch, 1984).

Examples of early approaches include William James's *Varieties of Religious Experience*, published in 1902 (1985) and Sigmund Freud's theories about the unconscious processes from which religion may have developed, published in 1909 and 1921 (1985a, b). James and Freud both located the causes of religion within individuals, although social contexts may play a more prominent role.

While questions about private religious experiences are still alive, contemporary psychologists usually look for data from quite large groups of people and not just from a few legendary or confirmative cases. What survives in psychology must be measurable. 'Will', for example, has disappeared from psychology (but not from ordinary discourse) because it cannot be measured, while 'intelligence' has remained an important concept because, although IQ tests are often criticized as not equally fair to those from different cultures or social environments, it can be measured.

Religion or 'religiousness' is hard to quantify because it is only made public in what believers say about themselves, in the claims they make, or in their conduct. Many people however, prefer to keep their religion hidden. Despite that, psychologists are expected to be able to find out why ideas about God differ so much and why they have such wide 'psychological' appeal. Depending on your perspective this is either an easy or a difficult problem. Religion, which has advocated both feasting and fasting, intoxication and prohibition, wealth and poverty, prostitution and chastity, is not a simple phenomenon. Any catalogue of what has been taught and made available by different religions is of little help in understanding it. Is a religious perspective simply something that we either have or don't have? If so, does it involve blind faith, outward conformity combined with private reservations about the doctrines that are offered, or a directly mystical experience of God? These are all in a sense private or covert states, but, like prayers, though they do not have to be made public they depend on a religious community to make them possible. While we might lack sympathy for those whose religion is different from ours (as in, 'While *you* worship God in *your* way, *we* worship God in *his*'), Christianity is not the only World Religion. Furthermore, the separate Christian traditions have their own emphases, while new religious movements and sceptics claim their own grounds for belief or disbelief, and some replace 'religion' itself with the perspectives of science or of materialism.

Psychology stands apart from those disputes. It brings a scientific attitude to the systematic study of religion. William James defined religion as what people do with their solitude. Robert Thouless identified it with the solutions (and the disputes) that its traditions have about 'the world as a whole'. How people make those received solutions their own (which some people seem unable to do) and how to build inner confidence, security and a sense of authenticity, are central religious and psychological questions, if we are not to be plagued with doubt until we confront the 'last things'. Not everyone can replace magic or childlike hope with a sacramental attitude. But how can we establish whether Aboriginal rain-dancers really expect material effects from their ritual or are simply using it to acknowledge their unity with nature? What are the other ways to understand the symbolic meaning of a ritual and assign value to it, especially when we are in a sense all equidistant from infinity?

We must try to bring at least two entirely different psychological approaches together in our study of religion. One involves the empirical data that captures what people know or do. The other draws on theory to interpret data from the actions of particular people or from the symbols they use (as in C. G. Jung's (1958) analysis of how the Mass transforms the material into the spiritual). These approaches can only discover the gods indirectly. A scientific attitude makes the transcendent appear immanent in the responses of those who are observed, or who report on what they are doing, thinking or feeling. Such outward projections too easily distort whatever has been experienced.

Does giving information to others ever reduce the immediacy of our own experiences or beliefs? How does the presence of other people influence our religious behaviour? Does a religion apply its own psychology in the rules it prescribes? Do religions rely for their success on giving emotional satisfaction? What appeal *do* religions have? How can those appeals be explained? Is religion losing its appeal? While you will not find specific answers to such questions in this book, I hope it will help you to examine them.

As well as looking at what is required for any psychological study of religion I shall discuss what is known about the religious behaviour of individuals and groups, about individuals' beliefs, attitudes and values, about the nature of the religious personality, and about conversion, change and religious development, and religious experience and commitment. The last chapters of the book consider current theories and some uses of the psychology of religion.

1 Religion and its Scientific Study

Since we are in the main not sceptics, we might go on and frankly confess to each other the motives of our several faiths. I frankly confess mine – I cannot but think that at the bottom they are of an aesthetic and not a logical sort. The 'through-and-through' universe seems to suffocate me with its infallible impeccable all-pervasiveness . . . rather as if I had to live in a large seaside boarding-house with no private bedroom in which I might take refuge.

William James, *Essays in Radical Empiricism*, pp. 267–8

> by the cold and religious
> we were taken in hand
> shown how to feel good
> and told to feel bad
> tongue tied and terrified
> we learned how to pray
> now our feelings run deep
> and cold as the clay.

Pink Floyd, 'The final cut'

People have been confessing and accounting for their religious faith for many centuries, and for many reasons. Some hope to bring others to their point of view, a few are filled with their own enthusiasm or conviction, which they use to produce greater intimacy in their spiritual search. About one hundred years ago psychologists began to look systematically at those accounts, not for their religious interest but as scientific data that might show what is involved in 'being religious'. In fact, psychological and social explanations have stood alongside other explanations of what people say and actually do since the earliest times. On the day of Pentecost, for example, those who began to speak with other tongues were mocked on the grounds that 'These men are full of new wine' (Acts 2.13). Psychologists are similarly practical. They resist more difficult theological or philosophical interpretations of behaviour, preferring solutions that can be settled by careful and systematic observations of the ways that, for example, alcohol or being in a crowd, influence our actions, beliefs and judgement of what is acceptable.

Explanations that are not derived from empirical evidence are more like the excuses we give to justify what we have done than the soundly based theories scientists strive to construct from their controlled experiments of what happens.

Systematic studies of religious experience had a firm place in modern psychology as it developed in the late nineteenth century. The first article on religion in a psychological journal, was by Leuba (1896) and reported a study of conversion; Starbuck wrote the first *Psychology of Religion* in 1899, William James's *Varieties of Religious Experience*, published in 1902, is still regarded as a classic in this field (cf. Gorsuch and Spilka, 1987). Its twenty chapters were given as the Gifford Lectures on Natural Religion at Edinburgh University in 1901 and 1902. An 'authoritative text' of this book was published by the Harvard University Press in 1985.

A little history

Many of the founders of modern psychology wrote about religion. While William James relied heavily on autobiographical and clinical material to support his argument that a psychological approach is essential for understanding religious experience, Wilhelm Wundt, who established the first psychological laboratory in 1879, was more concerned with the ways religion integrates (and is enforced by) groups, societies and cultures. (Emile Durkheim, who founded the modern sociology of religion, was one of Wundt's students.)

James wrote, 'The word "religion" cannot stand for any single principle or essence, but is rather a collective name for the specific ways it is possible to be recognised as "religious"' (1985, p. 30). He also noted that the 'religious sentiment' (an old-fashioned term now) has been variously aligned with a feeling of dependence, with a kind of fear, with 'love and the sexual life', and with an awareness of the infinite (p. 31). Such psychological interpretations of religion were not new even in 1902, and they reflect the variety of forms religion can take. Others would add an implicit *sense* of God, a response to the beauty of nature, and custom and habit to James's list. Some religious believers insist that religion does not depend on such states of mind or emotions, since the Creator exists outside and beyond, or within, all we know or can ever know.

Early investigators were especially interested in the different forms of religious response. They noted, for example, that while some people were converted quickly others seemed to grow slowly into the tradition they had always accepted. James contrasted those who were 'once-born' against the 'twice-born'. He also made a distinction between the religion of healthy-mindedness and that of the sick soul. James felt that all these different forms of religion were equally legitimate. While Starbuck had compared those who had had a sudden conversion involving an experience of an escape from sin with those who had struggled towards their religious ideal, William James noted that the once-born find the 'Romish Church . . . a more congenial soil to grow in than Protestantism, whose fashions of feeling have been set by minds of a decidedly pessimistic order' (1985, pp. 73–4).

During the 1920s psychology came to be defined as the 'scientific study of behaviour' rather than as 'the science of mental life' (cf. Miller, 1972). Psychologists began to give less attention to what people thought, believed or might say about themselves than to what could be directly observed about human behaviour (or of the behaviour of animals). A few psychologists interested in religion therefore turned their attention from descriptions of religious conversion, belief and experience to studies of religious behaviour in, for example, the depth of genuflection and the times of arriving for church services (see p. 27 below). Many others who had been interested in religion turned to counselling and pastoral work rather than to research. The study of religion became unfashionable and even a 'taboo topic' for psychologists during and after the 1930s (Farberow, 1963). A few, however, including Thurstone and Chave (1929) (see Table 3, p. 34 below), developed measures of religious attitudes in order to compare them with attitudes to other aspects of the social and political environment.

In the 1960s psychology changed direction again. The importance of the beliefs and aspirations of individuals in guiding their action and shaping their experiences became increasingly recognized. This cognitive perspective enabled psychologists to take religious beliefs and practices seriously again. They began to look at the religious differences between individuals and groups as instances of the ways personality, traditions, and social influences guide action.

Interest turned back to Gordon Allport's (1950) characterization of those who were extrinsically religious and rather consensual in their orientation, simply following the rules and using religion as a means to achieve their own ends of personal security or social gain. He had contrasted this orientation against those who were intrinsically religious and committed to the ideals of a religion as an end in itself, thereby transcending their own self-centredness (cf. Donahue, 1985). William James had earlier drawn a similar contrast between the tender-minded who are guided by religious principles, idealistic and optimistic, and the tough-minded, who are empiricist, individualistic, fatalistic and sceptical. Eysenck (1954) later linked that distinction to the contrast between liberal and conservative attitudes, and in his *Psychology of Politics* contrasted tough-minded conservatives (now called 'drys') against the tender-minded conservatives (the 'wets'), but also against the tough or tender-minded liberals (see also p. 5.

An important question we must examine is the value or the uses of these or other typological differences to identify various groups of people.

Most agree now that behaviourists, or the tough-minded empiricists, have rather different scientific and social attitudes from the more tender-minded psychologists who prefer to talk about theories rather than 'hard data' and who would use their theories to interpret the meaning of religious or other doctrines and symbols. C. G. Jung and Sigmund Freud are probably the best-known psychologists who have used their theories in that way. Jung (who gave the unconscious a more benign role than did Freud) was sympathetic to religion, perhaps because he was the son of a Lutheran pastor in Switzerland, while Freud was rather critical of many of its forms.

The psychology of religion is now primarily concerned with finding evidence to support, refute or revise accepted theories, and with developing new theories that clarify distinctions or classifications of religious individuals and groups. There are two important ways in which this can be done. One looks at the coherence of separate measures of religious and psychological characteristics across diverse groups of people. The other compares different well-defined groups – for example, men and women, or Catholics and Protestants – to find what it is that marks one group off from the other.

It might still be, however, that the most appropriate people for psychologists to study are those who have experienced a religious conversion, or who have deliberately chosen their religious allegiance. The beliefs of such people might be expected to fit their psychological characteristics or background more closely than the beliefs of those who have simply stayed in the religion or denomination they grew up in even though they may no longer have a strong conviction that it 'suits' them. Whatever group is studied an important question concerns the ways an individual does or does not fit religion into the rest of his or her life. Another question involves the extent to which the facts of religion are glossed or interpreted to reflect overriding religious, non-religious or anti-religious perspectives.

The origins of religion?

Until quite recently, many psychologists searched for the 'origins' of religion. One well-known explanation was developed by Freud, who argued that the basis of religious belief was to be found in the obsessive practices and ceremonials that control or suppress 'instinctual impulses'. That theory was published in 1907: by 1919 Freud (cf. Freud, 1985a,b) had broadened it to include an anthropological perspective

4

on the respect given to sacred and taboo objects, people or relationships, especially to the dead. He linked this attitude to primitive or pre-scientific thinking about the natural world.

Freud argued that 'the beginnings of religion, morals, society and art converge in the Oedipus complex' – in the unfulfilled and emotionally ambivalent sexual wishes that young children unconsciously direct to their parents. Freud claimed that these feelings are 'handled' by projecting some of our good and our bad feelings onto a deity (cf. Freud, 1985b, p. 219).

Freud's writing on religion, unlike that of Jung, is pervaded by the notion that religion involves essentially 'neurotic' behaviour, at both the individual and the cultural level. He wrote in *The Future of an Illusion*, 'religious ideas are teachings and assertions about facts and conditions of external (or internal) reality which tell one something one has not discovered for oneself and which lay claims to one's belief' (1985a, p. 206). And he looked to cultural phenomena for confirmation of the universal principles he detected in the lives of individuals.

Jung, though an early collaborator with Freud, later adopted a different view of religion. He saw the unconscious as a symbol of harmony rather than alienation, and acknowledged the independence and priority of religious belief and ritual. Jung wrote in 1937:

> Religion appears to me to be a peculiar attitude of mind which could be formulated in accordance with the original use of the word *religio*, which means a careful consideration and observation of dynamic factors conceived as 'powers', spirits, daemons, gods, laws, ideas, ideals, or whatever name man has given to such factors in his world as he has found powerful, dangerous or helpful enough to be taken into careful consideration, or grand, beautiful, and meaningful enough to be devoutly worshipped and loved. (1958, p. 8)

Other early theories about the origins of religion include reference to the bald power of nature and belief in its animation by personal spirits (Tylor, 1877), to the totemic powers of ancestors embodied in a group's identity (Durkheim, 1915), and to magical and religious control as a form of primitive science (Malinowski, 1925). All these analyses are highly theoretical, and although they were informally supported by observations and clinical experience systematic tests of those theories have not found the general support that was once claimed for them.

The concept of God

An important focus of this book is on methods of investigation, and the results of empirical tests of psychological theories about religion. For example, Freud's view that one's concepts of God involve projected images of one's father has been investigated by Vergote and Tamayo (1980, p. 12). The basic method they used involved sets of eighteen 'maternal' descriptions (including 'patient', 'warm' and 'sensitive') and eighteen 'paternal' descriptions (like 'strong', 'powerful', 'takes the initiative'). Each of these descriptions was rated first, for its relevance to one's actual parents and then as a representation of God. Three separate ideas of God were found, covering availability (which was the most important, accounting for 82% of the variance), firmness, and authority. That 'availability' factor was found to be aligned with parental tenderness, and was more maternal than paternal. The findings suggest that concepts of God are not uniquely male, and that Freud's argument disregarded the confusion among believers about God's character which, as Gorsuch (1968) shows, traditionally connotes glory and majesty but also involves God being companionable and benevolent, as well as wrathful, severe and avenging. (Some of these characteristics might also align with traditional doctrines about the Three Persons in the Trinity, which have been neglected in psychological studies of the concepts of God.)

The Christian conception of God has both female *and* male features. It is defined predominantly by what particular religious traditions emphasize, not by our own personality characteristics. Some individuals will, nevertheless, idiosyncratically use or talk about their images of God as if they related specifically to one or the other parent. Without a great deal of additional evidence it is unreasonable to assume that talk of God as father expresses an unusual psychopathology about one's natural father.

Several important points can be made from this work. Data that show group trends or differences cannot automatically be taken to apply to particular individuals. What a person says (or how they answer a questionnaire) may not be what they really mean to say. If, for example, someone uses what seem to be very concrete or animistic images in talking of God it could be only 'in a manner of speaking'. And if they do take religious language entirely literally we must still decide if those images involve 'infantile' or 'immature' attitudes, and, if they do, whether they should be purified and expressed in a way that is more psychologically 'mature', which, some might argue, might eventually require the 'death of God'. Others emphasize that a balanced and mature commitment that centres on 'faith in Christ' *is* possible (e.g. Godin, 1971, p. 147). Religious intentions may always be rather ambiguous.

Psychologies of religion

People obviously become religious for different reasons and in different ways, p. ix above. Underlying the various types of religious orientation lie assessments of whose (or which) religion can properly be judged as immature or unusual, and what the mature forms of religion might be like. Those evaluations depend quite explicitly on what any observer of (or participant in) religion assumes is 'proper', which will in turn depend on the influences, expectations and norms he or she has been exposed to. While there will be approved and disapproved forms of personal religion, I have noted that psychologists have not yet cashed in on the separate emphasis that each Person in the Trinity may be given, nor have they explained why the Father predominates in Unitarianism, or the Spirit in Pentecostalism, or why Roman Catholicism gives special devotion to Mary. Instead of pursuing the implications of those different perspectives psychologists have followed Fromm (1950), who distinguished authoritarian from humanistic orientations to religion, King and Hunt (1975), who distinguished literal and anti-literal from mythological perspectives, or Lenski (1961), who contrasted doctrinal orthodoxy and devotionalism.

William James (1902) gave weight to the religion of 'healthy-mindedness' which 'looks on all things and sees that they are good' (1985, p. 87) rather than to that of 'sick souls' who take the 'experience of evil as something essential' (p. 162). Proposing that a person's religion could be 'instinctual' (perhaps implanted by God), habitual or social, W. H. Clark (1958) identified three forms of religion, a primary religion based on 'an authentic inner experience of the divine combined with whatever efforts the individual may make to harmonise . . . with the divine' (p. 23), a secondary religion that is routine and based on obligation, and a tertiary form of religion that is accepted on another's authority.

Those separate forms of religious attachment seem to converge on emphases that can be summarized as predominantly closed and convergent or predominantly open and linked to continued growth or development, in which to be 'surprised by joy' (in the words of C. S. Lewis) is always possible. It is, however, not clear that even these two forms are necessarily linked to psychological differences in the personality or experience of individuals, although they do involve fundamental attitudes and preferences.

Although psychologists try to adopt a neutral attitude to the beliefs of those they study, it is sometimes hard for them to disregard completely their own religious and scientific convictions and put aside all the prejudices that influence judgements about which facts are important and what interpretation should be put on them. Judgements of the validity of, for example, a concrete belief in God's existence or of a particular mystical experience are themselves useful psychological data, since what for one person might be evidence for a religious solution can be a reason for another's apostasy. Such inconsistencies sustain our psychological interest as we gather information about what religious beliefs might 'mean' and how conclusions are reached by the supporters and opponents of particular doctrines and practices.

A 'religious psychology' is therefore based on assumptions about the truth of the doctrines of a particular tradition. It must be clearly distinguished from the 'psychology of religion' which is carried out within the constraints and assumptions of a scientific study of human behaviour. This distinction can be quite clearly seen by comparing reports in the *Journal of Psychology and Christianity* or the *Journal of Psychology and Theology* with those in the *Journal for the Scientific Study of Religion* or the *Review of Religious Research*. But while academic psychologists keep a 'scholarly distance' from the religious beliefs and practices they study, many of them also have a directly personal interest in religion. (A special number of the *Journal of Psychology and Christianity* for Summer 1986, 5(2), has statements about their work by fifteen influential psychologists, from academic and religious perspectives.)

Some psychologists have used religious processes as a vehicle to investigate social or psychological processes and attitudes rather than religion itself. A few still hope to use psychology to destroy religion. But religiously committed and scientifically controlled approaches to religion only come into conflict when science distorts or misrepresents religion or when a religious group resists any scientific examination, controls its own history, disallows contact with outsiders or forbids discussion of its doctrines.

A few general findings

The psychology of religion is now primarily concerned with the social and personal correlates of religious practice and belief. It has been found, for example, that religious denomination as well as age, sex and occupation can define one's identity as a person, and that parents are a critical influence in forming positive religious attitudes. Those who are married have the lowest levels of church attendance, though parents with young children tend to be over-represented amongst church-goers. Church attendance declines between the ages of 18 and 30, but peaks again after the age of 50. Women are more 'religious' than men by every criterion, including church membership, church attendance, prayer, religious belief, mystical experience and religious attitudes. Despite these consistencies, there are great differences in the levels of church attendance not only between those in the main denominations (and especially between Catholics, those in main-line Protestant groups, and members of small sects) but also between believers in different countries. Church-going is, for example, more common in the United States than it is in the United Kingdom.

To accept religious doctrines or perspectives depends more on social definitions of what is required of a 'religious' person than on any psychological characteristics. Thus, women seem to be more religious than men. There is no strong evidence that those in different religious groups have particular personality characteristics, despite a popular belief that that is the case. Religion has been shown to have largely positive effects on personal adjustment, and it has been demonstrated, for example, that acute stress can be relieved by prayer. Those who participate in religious activities are more likely to avoid extra-marital sex and 'substance abuse', and those who are deeply religious are likely to be less prejudiced than those who are more casually religious. (Such generalizations, which are drawn from the work of Argyle and Beit-Hallahmi (1975) and Spilka, Hood and Gorsuch (1985), have of course to be qualified in specific cases.)

While psychologists are fascinated by the reasons for the uneven distribution of religious beliefs between people, sociologists are more interested in the effects of religious organizations on their members and the nature of the sacred–profane distinction. Opinion polls have therefore become an important source of data for sociologists of religion. By using similar questions they can show how religious beliefs have changed since 1936, when the first of Gallup's surveys were done, and how they vary with age, sex and occupation, or religious denomination. A recent poll (Abrams, Gerard and Timms, 1985, p. 61) showed that 58 per cent of a British sample identified themselves as 'religious', 50 per cent agreed with the statement, 'God is important in my life' and 50 per cent agreed they 'need moments of prayer'. Nineteen per cent said they have had a 'spiritual experience', 34 per cent said they often 'think about the meaning and purpose of life', and 50 per cent said they never 'think life is meaningless'. (Unfortunately the report does not say how much these groups over-lap.) Those results can be compared with the findings of a Gallup Poll carried out in European countries in June 1981, where 14 per cent in Britain, compared to a mean of 25 per cent in Europe, said they go to church at least once a week. But a far greater proportion in Britain than in the rest of Europe accepted the Ten Commandments as applying to them and 78 per cent in Britain agreed that 'Thou shalt not commit adultery' (though interestingly, only 25 per cent said they obey it) compared to 48 per cent in France. 'Keep holy the Sabbath' was the commandment least widely accepted in Britain (22 per cent), the next being not to take the Lord's name in vain (42 per cent). To have no other gods was accepted by 45 per cent. The other commandments, which had been phrased by the questioners to emphasize their moral implications, were accepted by at least 78 per cent, which suggests that British people are more concerned with the social than the divine aspects of religion. While a majority in the British sample believed that all the commandments applied to them, most said they doubted that others adhered to them. Despite that, 76 per cent said they believe in God and 75 per cent believe in heaven.

The questions in these kinds of surveys are too bald to be able to explore what is understood by such religious terms as 'heaven' and whether, for example, it is God's dwelling place or involves a personal destiny. A survey among 151 people in 'senior positions' in Britain reported in the *Spectator* on 13 December 1986 found that 86 per cent said they believe that Christ's miracles actually happened, 85 per cent believe that Jesus is the Son of God, 82 per cent believe in the Trinity, 81 per cent in heaven and 80 per cent believe that prayer can alter events on earth.

Psychological interpretations

When general trends like these are fully analysed they reveal the Christian consensus in Britain, and can be used to identify the social and demographic factors which influence people to become and remain, to resist or to give up being religious believers. While most psychologists probably study religion because of its traditional role in social life there are close links between the concern of psychology *and* of religion with guilt, desire, sin, and the control of behaviour, although not necessarily in those exact terms. Psychological concepts like projection, suggestion, learning or habit have been used to understand religion, but also to explain it away, while religious concepts like sin, conversion and commitment have been used as models of more general social alignments. To take belief, practice and experience as the cornerstones of religion gives a correspondence with thought, action and feeling (or cognition, behaviour and affect), and with the primary psychological categories which St Augustine had identified as reason, will and memory.

Sociologists avoid psychological explanations, suggesting instead that belief in God gives plausible answers to existential questions about the social (and moral) order, when for example, it holds that injustice in this world can be rectified in the next. Holding religious beliefs may, however, give self-fulfilling guarantees of the effects they offer, although religious people also claim that the doctrines they accept are true statements about God and the world. We encounter there the problem of the perspective from which any observations are made: observers are expected to remain detached while recognizing the involvement believers have with their beliefs. Believers may be so involved with what they believe that they reject any psychological explanation of their faith as unnecessary – even offensive – because of the reductionism it seems to imply. To ask people about their religious beliefs sometimes seems to them like questioning their reality or their truthfulness. Furthermore, Robert Thouless (1935) showed that while most people are quite ready to express uncertainty about matters of fact which are in principle empirically verifiable, like whether or not there are tigers in China, religious statements such as 'There is a hell in which the wicked will be punished', do not draw uncertainty but great confidence in their truth *or* falsity. Wittgenstein (1970, p. 53) illustrated the point with a philosophical anecdote:

> Suppose someone were a believer and said: 'I believe in a Last Judgement,' and I said: 'Well, I'm not so sure. Possibly.' You would say that there is an enormous gulf between us. If he said: 'There is a German aeroplane overhead,' and I said: 'Possibly. I'm not so sure,' you'd say we were fairly near. It isn't a question of my being anywhere near him, but on an entirely different plane, which you could express by saying: 'You mean something altogether different, Wittgenstein!'

These differences also show up in explanations of the meaning of propositions. Unshakeable beliefs are supported by an appeal to the facts, by reasoning, and by the ways they regulate a believer's life, with the risks from falsification that entails. While such solid beliefs are stable, it is not yet clear how they become established beyond appeals to authority, tradition, experience or by empirical tests.

Psychologists who treat beliefs, or claims about them, as variables that are to be explained may also be concerned with their links to social and psychological factors that include the support they are given by a group and by other believers' confidence or satisfaction with them. Such meanings and claims can also be taken as dependent variables in studies of the ways religious beliefs reflect a parent's religious commitment, or the believer's age or sex.

When beliefs are held strongly they can be used to regulate one's life and shape interactions with other people. We will see later that knowing a person's religious beliefs allows predictions to be made about that person's attitude to issues such as gambling, censorship and so on. Indeed, trying to understand the sometimes uncanny correspondence between religious and non-religious responses is one of the things that keeps interest in the psychology of religion alive. The design of any study will, however, depend on the hypotheses that are to be tested. This assumes a well-formulated theory and enough prior information to make systematic tests worthwhile. Scientific understanding grows by forming conjectures, or theories, that can be tested experimentally and then revising them (or the whole approach) in the light of the results of that experiment.

Theology and psychology

Many people who say they only accept what they can directly verify by their own experience have had difficulty taking religion seriously. (This was the problem that confronted Thomas after the resurrection, see John 20.24–9.) That view, however, disregards the intangibility of all the other secondary or derived knowledge that we take on trust, especially about science. And many believers *do* base their faith on compelling experiences – of God, or of a unity that is hard to put into words, especially in times of crisis or repose. While some reject those experiences as illusory, about one-third of the population report having had them (cf. David Hay, 1982, and below, p. 90).

It may be too much to hope that when people do not recognize their own experience in a psychological account, they will not simply reject it but ask themselves why that psychological analysis seems invalid. Such informed criticism could help to broaden our psychological approaches. Instead of leaving the systematic study of God to theology and the study of religious practice and belief to psychology, we should aim for an integration of theology and psychology in understanding the ways religious doctrines come to be accepted.

Although theology works within its own assumptions, it has not been immune to psychological or other influences. As Maurice Wiles (1976) pointed out, 'The theologian cannot ignore the findings of the natural scientist because in elucidating the nature of the world we inhabit the scientist is elucidating the nature of what is part of the theologian's subject matter.' The work of psychologists and sociologists, he adds, offers 'a perspective on human life which is of the utmost importance for the theologian to grasp. Its bearing on theology may be indirect, but it is also very profound' (p. 79).

Psychology certainly has relevance for moral theology, which examines the relation of Christian and other beliefs to moral and religious problems, for dogmatic theology, which is concerned with the doctrines and authorities that form the basis for the religious beliefs and opinions of individuals, for natural theology, with its interest in religious experience and action, and for practical or pastoral theology, which examines the interaction between belief and behaviour in religious formation and in adult life. And 'Religious Studies', which has recently developed as the academic study of religion in general and of the different perspectives embodied in the world's religions, also has a direct interest in how psychological and social processes shape religious experience, cultures and their history.

But even William James emphasized that he could not hope to cover the whole field of religion. He therefore restricted his analysis to the 'varieties of religious experience', leaving out questions about institutional religion, particular religious doctrines, the history of religions, and the religions of non-western or traditional societies, which anthropologists have dealt with. Although psychologists focus on the personal aspects of religion they must also keep in mind the social institutions and traditions that shape the doctrines and practices to which individuals respond.

It is no longer fashionable to draw analogies between religion and fetishism (the worship of inanimate objects), superstition or magic. 'Primitive' religions are no longer contrasted with Christianity as 'lower' forms of religion. While real sacrifices might have been replaced by symbolic or sacramental rites of 'praise and thanksgiving', not everyone agrees that Christian worship is more sophisticated because of that. But psychologists have not yet come to grips with non-Christian religions, except for a few studies that have examined the practice of meditation in Eastern religious traditions (West, 1987) and some work on the way religious cosmologies and doctrines embody their own psychological and social theories. The assumption that scientific knowledge has eliminated the need for religious ideas to account for what cannot yet be understood is also unfashionable.

While some would restrict 'religion' to existential questions about the meaning of life or the nature of death, others would widen its use to include a compelling interest in sport, money, or politics. To assert that religion attracts those who are psychologically immature inevitably reduces all religious claims to childlike errors. But even that might be seen as an ambiguous interpretation, since Christians are taught that they must become like children if they are to enter the Kingdom (see Matthew 18.3).

Religion defined

William James defined religion in terms of 'the feelings, acts and experiences of individual men [and, we need to add, women] in their solitude, so far as they apprehend themselves to stand in relation to whatever they may consider the divine' (1985, p. 34). That relationship, he went on to say, may be moral, physical or ritual. In a reaction against James's explicit disregard of the social and the cultural relevance of religion Robert Thouless (1971) defined religion as 'a felt practical relationship with the divine'. Neither of these perspectives acknowledges the tension between what people think or believe privately and what they are prepared to reveal about that or how they show religion in their lives. Individuals themselves have to hold their religious beliefs and other actions together, and every religious tradition, despite (or because of) its clearly specified standards and expectations, has difficulty controlling its members.

William James unjustly excluded Buddhism and other systems that do not necessarily include belief in God (or gods) from his definition of religion. Nevertheless, transcendental or transpersonal systems, including some of the 'new religious movements', recognize an abstract power (rather than a personal God), or a sense of identity, that extends beyond individuals. Those who draw on Jungian psychology and eastern thought might also argue that western ideas about God are not crucial for many of the transcendental implications or attitudes that 'religion' implies. As William James said: 'It makes a tremendous emotional and practical difference to one whether one accepts the universe in the drab discoloured way of stoic resignation to necessity, or with the passionate happiness of Christian saints' (1985, p. 41).

Any religious orientation is, however, supported by some social context and tradition, and when people are encouraged to express their deeper feelings, what they say often conflicts with other norms about how to preserve the social order. Psychologists have been more concerned with these aspects of life and its values, than with beliefs in specific doctrines, although what is believed to be 'religious' may have implications for other attitudes and beliefs, especially when doctrines, about eternal life, for example, are interpreted literally. It has also been found that a knowledgeable insider's perspective on religion will yield different conclusions from those of a detached observer. Those who are religiously involved or committed also have a more differentiated understanding of religion than most outsiders. Yet both perspectives are valid, and one task for the psychology of religion could be to show how each of them develops, and the effects they have.

The psychology of religion might seem rather confusing because it attempts to bring disparate perspectives together and because its conclusions may conflict with established presuppositions – if, for example, as those in some religions do, one hopes to change society by changing its individual members rather than the rules.

A primary contribution of modern psychology has been the development of methods and procedures that allow replicable measures of the characteristics of individuals and groups to test specific theories or hypotheses. Any psychology of religion must be built on data gathered by using such methods. Those who assert that religion is not a proper field for psychological analysis are either too protective of religion, perhaps for fear that it might be questioned, or because they believe that the truth has already been completely revealed, or are restrictive in what they will allow psychology to investigate. There are good grounds for criticizing the superficiality of some of the psychological studies of religion, because of the limited samples of people who have been investigated or the unreal and invalid data that were gathered. Despite that, one hopes that progress will continue to be made in understanding religion and how it is used by different individuals. The best psychological work has already enriched our understanding by clarifying what it means in psychological terms to be 'religious'.

The components of religion

Psychologists are broadly agreed that the elements of any personal religion draw together:

1. knowledge of particular doctrines and practices concerning some transcendental order;
2. beliefs or disbeliefs, attitudes and values about the truth or falsity, and the credibility, of those doctrines;
3. experiences that give authenticity to some direct awareness of reality;
4. behaviour or practice (and action) in rituals, sacraments, and in other ways that ensure involvement with a transcendental order;
5. social contexts and situations that allow and validate religion;
6. secular consequences and implications of a religious alignment (including the effects on honesty, sexual behaviour and chastity).

The first three of these components are more covert and protected than the other three, which are necessarily public. This is a crucial distinction both for psychology and for religion, although one or the other mode is usually emphasized, as when behaviourists disregard the mental processes behind behaviour, or when cognitive psychologists measure the use of mental images or reactions to pain. People who stress the objective factors in either religion or psychology tend to be more closely aligned with a politically conservative position than are those primarily concerned with what is subjective.

A complete analysis of religion must recognize the following features, which King (1986) has identified:

1. a social tradition or culture that supports and interprets a cosmology with deities, and saints or spirits;
2. sacred knowledge that is to be passed on to those who have been approved to receive it;
3. techniques by which spiritual power can be found, and used appropriately in prayer, sacraments, blessing or ritual;
4. actors, believers or adherents, who align the meaning of life with a set of religious practices, ideas, or doctrines, and so carry the religion;
5. fellowship, or communication with other believers, and with the transcendental world.

This list, which roughly parallels the psychological components of religion, contrasts the people in a religion against the religious system itself. Table 1 gives a schematic summary of those sets of components to emphasize the way they correspond.

TABLE 1

Aligning the features of any religion with the elements studied psychologically

Religions involve . . .	Psychology studies . . .
a. a tradition	1. knowledge of a tradition
b. sacred knowledge	2. belief
c. spiritual techniques and rituals	3. experience
d. adherents or members	4. behaviour
e. within-group fellowship	5. social contexts
	6. secular consequences

Summary

This book aims to show how psychology has dealt with religion, and the conclusions it has reached about it. Questions yet to be answered are distinguished from those that psychologists have either settled or discarded, and from the theories that build on verified conclusions or that might be starting points for the future. I assume that belief, experience and behaviour are the central features in any expression of a religion. When they are used appropriately they can achieve personal, social, and religious goals. This alone warrants the psychological study of religion.

My approach accepts that some religious claims rest on experiences of what appears sacred or mysterious, and are not necessarily signs of maladjustment or mere fantasies, especially when they recognize a 'creative impulse'. Van Gogh remarked that he could quite well dispense with God, but not with 'something greater than myself, something that is my whole life: the power of creation'. Such confidence contrasts with a sense of 'dryness' or idleness, as if creativity is impossible and 'God is dead', leaving only the 'dark night of the soul'. Such descriptions or explanations inform the data for systematic analyses and for the tests of our theories or speculations. Testable propositions include William James's assertion that religious experience 'spontaneously and inevitably engenders myths, superstitions, dogma, creeds, and metaphysical theologies, and criticisms of one set of these by the adherents of another'. Religious people, who may appear to be controlled *or* emotional, have their own perspectives on the priorities they give to their experience, belief and faith, to their own practice or to the formal sanctions of others. While individuals may be lost in, or set against, a religious system they have seldom just 'thought up' for themselves what it is they believe: it must be 'found' or received.

2 A Patterned but Illusory World

In psychology there are experimental methods and conceptual confusions.
L. Wittgenstein, *Philosophical Investigations*, 1958, p. 11

The eighteenth-century rationalists took for granted our immediate knowledge of God, as well as a finite intelligence and consciousness. The empiricists at that time, however, argued that knowledge of God, of the world and of ourselves has to be built up from sensory experience. Although we cannot hope to solve those philosophical puzzles, they emphasize the important distinction between knowledge and experience. A similar contrast between insiders' and outsiders' perspectives on what religions involve and the meaning they carry helps us to understand why direct involvement with a religion is necessary for a detailed analysis of it (see p. ix above).

To rely on empirical data and experience rather than on abstract theories and explanations is not simply a matter of preference. It involves a sharp difference of approach to problems. But while most psychologists are empiricists, there are still underlying disagreements between them about the innate capacities that allow us to process 'information' about the outside world, and go beyond the evidence of our senses to make judgements and decisions – which can range from whether or not to go to church next Sunday to whether or not to accept Christ as Saviour.

It is unlikely that observation alone could ever allow us to decide that men and women have an essential 'sense of God', because of the long western tradition that has argued about the nature and the reasons for religious experiences, and which has often identified religiousness as a skill, trait, habit or 'defect' (cf. John Bowker, 1973). Rudolf Otto's *Idea of the Holy* (1923), which gave us 'numinous' as a stronger word than 'religious', is the best developed argument that there is a natural, direct understanding of God. An alternative view holds that any sense of God derives indirectly from psychological processes such as compensation for weakness, resolution of guilt and anxiety, or the consolation for material or social deprivation. These views about the psychological basis of religion all stress its adaptive, and often its negative, role rather than the way religion contributes to self-realization, finding a positive ideal, encouraging creativity, or what Polanyi (1958, p. 285) called the 'passionate search for God'. All

18

these views contrast observers' or sceptics' attacks on the arrogance of religion with the support of those who have placed their confidence in it.

Empirical approaches

Like the earlier empiricists, we should clarify our assumptions about how anybody makes sense of the world and comes to terms with nature before considering the ways religion has been studied. Psychologists usually accept that we are all aware of our independence and selfhood, that we believe we have some control over our lives, and that as we reflect on our states of mind we think beyond ourselves to the natural and social environments with which we interact. While we *might* be rather egocentric and refer any judgement back to our own perspective, most people are detached or decentred enough to recognize that others may not reach conclusions similar to their own and that it is reasonable to respect some social consensus about many, if not all, issues. Although that conclusion itself goes beyond the evidence, we are constantly filling the inevitable gaps in our awareness, experience and knowledge of the world in whatever ways seem most appropriate, although disputes about our areas of autonomy will continue. A good and stable patterning of the world seems to be the most adaptive, even if we realize we are being misled as we accept it.

One particular problem in understanding religion concerns the extent to which we may be unaware of the ways we are set or 'primed' to reach conclusions that fit with our implicit wishes, hopes, or prior beliefs about what is or is not 'out there'. In arguing for the existence of angels, flying saucers, demons, taboos, and even of God, we may not realize *how* we have reached our conclusions. We may have simply accepted arguments that are consistent with our own or others' prejudices. So, for example, Norman Feather (1964) showed that when religious and non-religious people were asked to evaluate the logical validity of syllogisms, some pro- and some anti-religious in their conclusions, their evaluations were more congruent with their existing attitudes than with the logical truth or falsity of the syllogisms. One of the pro-religious syllogisms that the non-religious tended to reject, even though the conclusion follows validly from the premises, stated that,

> People who are without religion are spiritually devoid and need Christian teaching to show them the true way of life. Atheists and agnostics are people without religion and devoid of spiritual life. Therefore, atheists and agnostics need Christian teaching to show them the true way of life.

Any careful observer knows that it is easy to be misled in the interpretation of evidence by wishful thinking, or the *hope* that God exists. Some people claim to base their religious beliefs on a revelation or, as with Pascal's wager, a decision that the cost of being wrong about the existence of God far outweighs the benefits of being correct about it. The ambiguity of the evidence that supports belief in the existence of God is emphasized by the implausibility to many people of the classical arguments for God's existence, all of which have been questioned at one time or another. Although I do not know of any detailed psychological studies of this, when I have asked students what evidence they rely on for their belief in the existence of God, the patterned coherence of the world or an argument from design seems to carry the most weight.

Perceptual analogies

The argument that God gives coherence to our experience is analogous to resolving ambiguous patterns and visual illusions. Figures 1 and 2 are examples of the way interpretations must go well beyond the visual information that is given if we are to find plausible 'solutions' to each of those patterns. On the other hand, we find that it is almost impossible to make any coherent pattern from the random set of dots in Figure 3.

Finding the meaning in visual patterns might have a parallel in 'finding God'. Freud wrote in *The Future of an Illusion* (1985a, p. 198) that the store of ideas in religion were 'born from man's need to make his helplessness tolerable and built up from the material of memories of the helplessness of his own childhood and the childhood of the human race'. Freud maintained that religious and other doctrines are 'in their psychological nature, illusions' (p. 215), in the sense of being wished-for solutions to truly ambiguous stimuli. 'Fundamentally,' he wrote, 'we find only what we need and see only what we want to see' (*New Introductory Lectures*, 1933, p. 640). (The theory that perceptual processes are motivated in this way and are not realistic is now considered rather old-fashioned.)

Freud's extreme, but highly influential, analysis of the emotional basis of religion is broadly similar to a theory of Jean Piaget, the Swiss developmental psychologist, who in an essay on children's philosophies (1933) showed that young children postulate external causes beyond the world of appearances to explain how the clouds move and how other natural effects are produced. Yet adults who 'know' that childish explanations are wrong because they do not correspond with what is generally accepted to be the case may still offer them back to

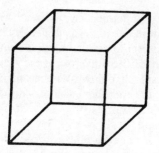

Fig. 1. *A Necker cube, the first visually ambiguous figure to have been described.*

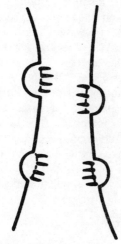

Fig. 2. *These could be meaningless marks, or a bear behind a tree.*

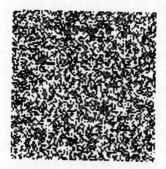

Fig. 3. *A Julesz random dot pattern.*

children or play imaginatively with them themselves. Western thought is often assumed to show a similar development to that of a child's growing understanding of the world, with the view that the earth is at the centre of the universe (as each child sees itself at the centre of its own world) changing to a heliocentric model, and then to a recognition that there are other solar systems. But our horizons do not necessarily expand. Wordsworth saw that 'Shades of the prison-house begin to close upon the growing boy.'

A different analysis of developing awareness would leave all questions about nature to science, and questions about morality or values to religion. While – the argument goes – scientific questions are settled empirically, with reference to the facts, religious truths depend on appeals to authority, whether in scripture, the Church, reason, or experience. But science and religion each have their own orthodoxies that are hard to override or change. Those who question received theories are too easily dismissed as deluded or paranoid. When, for example, people claim encounters with dead relatives, such claims can be 'tamed' by being described as 'a dream' or distanced by saying, 'It was *as if* someone was standing beside me.' Experiences can always be described in different ways, and the language we use to support a claim to vivid experiences is a crucial determinant of how others will react to our experience, and even to us as individuals. A consensus of meaning or explanation is essential if we are to maintain a stable social world, and continue to interact with others. But that consensus, preserved (and carried) by our linguistic and social rules, can become a strait-jacket that is hard to escape.

Science and religion

While the scientists' consensus is always being reconstructed, they are constrained because their theories must be tested against the findings from systematic observations of natural processes. Religious doctrines, however, are constrained by the traditions that those in authority preserve and use to attack those who would challenge them, and to a lesser extent by the social contexts within which they are being used.

Psychologists concentrate on theories which stress the way religions satisfy our need for meaning or allay fear in the face of suffering and death or focus apparently irrational experiences (as when Job says, 'Though he slay me, yet will I trust in him', 13.15). Quite recently many psychologists have become directly interested in the nature and functions of those explanations or attributions and theories themselves. So, instead of just explaining the origins of belief in God in terms of our need to have a stable world, or with reference to the ways we are upset when our life is shattered by untoward events, or by asserting that personal faith and a fear of death are linked, psychologists interested in attribution theory ask why those *theories* were formed, and how they came to be accepted.

The general belief appears to be that God is responsible for good outcomes, while people themselves are to be blamed for bad actions and outcomes (such as the consequences of refusing to help after an accident). Beliefs about God's action in the world therefore seem to be quite circumscribed. Although this is a recent research interest, it makes classical arguments for the existence of God look like any other attribution or explanation. To argue that God (or the Devil) put many things into the world to tempt, confuse or divert our attention inevitably raises impossible questions about our native character, and about whether we could ever think logically or solve problems directly. But the impossible drawing in Figure 4 does not have a stable solution: how it looks always depends on where your attention is focused. That, however, unlike many religious decisions, is independent of any moralism, blame or guilt about the goals that we have aimed at.

Thouless's *Psychology of Religion* (1923) examined the role of natural, moral, affective, and rational elements in religion, which he distinguished from unconscious processes and dispositions. In a new edition of that book in 1971 Thouless altered his terms, and identified natural, moral, emotional, and the intellectual as well as social factors in religion. Argyle (1958) also proposed a set of indirect psychological roots for religion that included guilt, need satisfaction, compensation, repression, social learning, and social benefits, which can be expedient and instrumental or expressive. But none of those factors pays enough attention to the way religious beliefs are made available to the

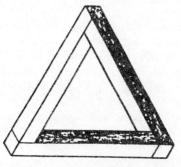

Fig. 4. *Penrose's impossible triangle.*

members of a community, who then develop their own religious beliefs or disbeliefs within that context.

Other theories that have been offered focus on the ways religious behaviour and belief is 'chunked', as computer experts might say, into theoretically separate 'bits'. Those chunks can involve high-level units like God as the creator, designer or sustainer, or they can use low-level units that break the big patterns down to the meaning of specific doctrines, to the decision to act in a particular way as a consequence of conversion or coercive persuasion, or to fit in with social rules and with what is expected as part of growing up.

Explanations

We do not try to explain why people accept the almost transcendental theories of modern physics or astronomy in psychological terms. Perhaps this is because we accept the wisdom of physicists or know how hard it is to understand their theories and intangible concepts. We also disregard, or do not know about, the disagreements physicists have amongst themselves. Yet we often try to offer psychological explanations of why people hold religious beliefs. This suggests that we think we know about religion, and do not treat it like science.

Experts' opinions in any field of work or study are the best guides to what is expected there. Whenever those opinions are systematically explored, to discover what they mean, they are given some social recognition. In a similar way, accepted attitudes to religion assume some implicit social support for them. Even the most careful observations can never resolve questions about false or true gods or whether religious attitudes should be purified of their 'primitive' psychological components, since they involve questions about values, and well-designed research can help to distinguish between competing explanations.

Explanations of the success of religious persuaders and evangelists, who rely on their own strong appeal or the credibility of their message, draw on theories of mind and of religion that will either support or reject religion itself. When concepts like 're-education' and 'de-programming' are used to attack or change what is disapproved of in religion, the same techniques that can humiliate or confuse one's identity may have been employed to set up whatever alignment is being challenged. While some people emphasize freedom of belief and of choice, others may use one of the other forms of direct behavioural control to change another's perspective or beliefs.

These are not new phenomena, for Christian martyrs have shown that to sacrifice their body emphasizes a mental or spiritual commitment to their beliefs that is stronger than mere conformity to imposed demands. But every religious practice depends on what is tolerated and judged to be possible, either psychologically or within particular social and religious groups, whether they belong to the new or old religions. That returns us to theology, ideology, and our own perspectives, since it seems easier to see the mote in another's eye than the beam in one's own. And does it matter *how* someone comes to the truth (which itself may be judged in relation to one's own position) so long as principles of independence, justice and honesty are maintained? One aim of counselling or therapy is therefore to help people form consistent beliefs about themselves, without assuming that those to be helped must be 'persuadable' or 'suggestible'.

Although we are better at identifying the negative than the positive states of mind, it is agreed that to make sense of life we require:

a. positive self-regard, and an ability to maintain this even when our faults are emphasized;

b. rewarding relationships with other people;

c. social groups (but especially a family) that provide help and support;

d. engagement with the wider society in work and leisure, and enough money to survive;

e. myths, metaphors and dreams that help us make sense of life itself;

f. an impetus to 'growth and development' that avoids restricted orthodoxies, closed-mindedness, cynicism and pathological doubt.

We have seen that studies of visual processes show the importance of finding meaning, the difficulties of 'seeing' or getting things straight, and the 'constructed' nature of the world we live in. Solutions to those and other problems influence how we adapt to our environment, even when the things we respond to may not be clear enough to us to elicit a firm response. In a similar way, we must adapt to numinous or spiritual interpretations or explanations as much as to our material circumstances.

Our sensitivity to the numinous, like our awareness of the material world, is easily dulled: although an engine-driver 'sees' that the rails ahead converge, previous experience, and an awareness or knowledge of parallel lines, makes it obvious to him that this is a false impression. If we lived in a weightless environment our conclusions from sensory information would not be the same as they are now. By analogy, our beliefs about God and religion (and even some of our 'rational' decisions about them) depend on the matrix of space and time within which they are to be evaluated. Questions about what the void was like before God created all things, or what lies beyond our universe, can only be answered in terms of some appropriate assumptions: these questions are no less valid because of that, even when they cannot be answered scientifically. It is odd, however, that we have much better information about the structure of the universe than about how the brain functions, or about mind and consciousness. While the mind and the universe are both very complex, like the engine-driver we must be pragmatic and limit our horizons if we are to work effectively within them. Although the physics and the economics of railways are irrelevant to most engine-drivers' efficiency, their state of mind is not.

Religious constraints

In the same sense, we can look at religion practically, or existentially, scientifically and theoretically. While some psychologists are more like practitioners than scientists when they examine religion for its traces of God, they are scientists when they look for the principles that guide the interaction between our physical and social worlds, within which people and their traditions create 'illusionistic' solutions from what is available to them and from their own (autistic) ideas, with an imagination that is constrained by the *rules* governing what can be 'said' and 'done' in particular contexts.

Explicit rules for, and the constraints on, religion include doctrines and rubrics for the conduct of church services. The implicit social rules for religion have not yet been accurately specified, though Allport (1934) showed that the time of arrival at church, depth of genuflection and belief in God conform to a J-shaped distribution (see Fig. 5). A psychological analysis of religious rules must identify those that should not be broken, the latitude allowed to those that can be changed and the rules that *are* being changed, such as those that relate to the roles women can play in the Church. Children are allowed to make mistakes and to ask many questions that are disallowed to adults: the elderly are exempted from rules about kneeling (in those traditions that apply them), while Catholics, Protestants and Jews share some rules (and doctrines), but not others. A few rules are obligatory only for some people (such as clergy) in each of those traditions.

When Thouless distinguished Christian doctrines that are orthodox and obligatory from general religious beliefs, and from those that are optional (like a belief in angels) he pointed up an important facet of

Opposite: Fig. 5. *Floyd Allport's (1934) J-curve distributions for making the sign of the cross, arrival at church and belief in God.*

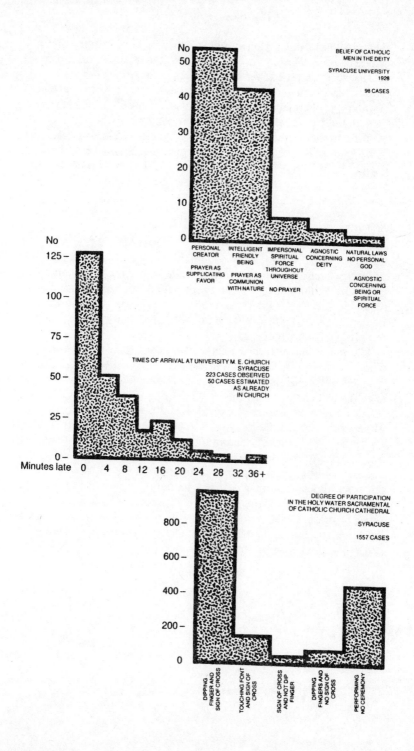

BELIEF OF CATHOLIC
MEN IN THE DEITY

SYRACUSE UNIVERSITY
1926

98 CASES

PERSONAL CREATOR

PRAYER AS SUPPLICATING FAVOR

INTELLIGENT FRIENDLY BEING

PRAYER AS COMMUNION WITH NATURE

IMPERSONAL SPIRITUAL FORCE THROUGHOUT UNIVERSE

NO PRAYER

AGNOSTIC CONCERNING DEITY

NATURAL LAWS NO PERSONAL GOD

AGNOSTIC CONCERNING BEING OR SPIRITUAL FORCE

TIMES OF ARRIVAL AT UNIVERSITY M. E. CHURCH
SYRACUSE
223 CASES OBSERVED
50 CASES ESTIMATED
AS ALREADY
IN CHURCH

Minutes late   0   4   8   12   16   20   24   28   32   36+

DEGREE OF PARTICIPATION
IN THE HOLY WATER SACRAMENTAL
OF CATHOLIC CHURCH CATHEDRAL

SYRACUSE

1557 CASES

DIPPING FINGER AND SIGN OF CROSS

TOUCHING FONT AND SIGN OF CROSS

SIGN OF CROSS AND NOT DIP FINGER

DIPPING FINGERS AND NO SIGN OF CROSS

PERFORMING NO CEREMONY

religious conformity. Conventions (or rules) about dress, diet and religious orders constrain and identify the modes and forms of religiousness and specify obligations that range from enforceable laws (about blasphemy, for example), through morality, to matters of etiquette. Judgements about those who break any of these rules can be more telling psychologically than observations of the ways people conform to them. But we do not know why, for example, the majority of people break the expected link between religious belief and behaviour by believing in God but not going to church. Nor do we know exactly how those who break that link would justify it.

Summary

Every explanation of religion derives from current fashions of thought. Their wide variety shows that it is easy to interpret and re-interpet religion when trying to understand what lies behind it. But, like religion itself, these explanations depend on social or ideological contexts that prescribe the 'knowledge' required for particular purposes, so that religion can be treated as just another theory, or as the embodiment of truth.

Those who have studied religion have used their own criteria for what it entails: William James stressed religious feelings, Robert Thouless concentrated on consciousness and Michael Argyle looked at religious behaviour. In this chapter I have emphasized the coherence of our experience and the rules (and conventions) for religion. Others have argued that religion is to be understood in a 'spread-out' sense that would include Communism, or even a consuming interest in football. Those broad usages are neglected in this book, as are comparisons between religion and superstition, myth, custom, secular ceremonies, and magic. That limitation might make western religious categories of the sacred seem narrow when compared with those of other social or religious traditions. Despite that, religious belief, experience, and practice can transform reality, at least for some people and for the groups to which they belong.

3 Religious Measures

Take ye the sum of all the congregation of the children of Israel, after their families, by the house of their fathers, with the number of their names, every male by their polls.

Numbers 1.2

The primary sources for the data on which empirical theories and explanations of religion rest are in the descriptions people give of their own knowledge and beliefs, attitudes, practice, and experience. When that information is combined and summarized for various groups the results are interpreted in relation to what else is known and understood about religion. Because so much of religious practice is prescribed and regularly repeated, simple observations of religious behaviour are likely to give less useful information about how any religion is accepted than what people say they believe, how they react to whatever they are expected to believe, and the meanings they find or give for their religious actions. Even then, what is said about religion tells us little without some knowledge of the norms of the groups to which religious people belong. That information is essential before we can conclude that religion is personally, rather than socially, adaptive or bizarre.

Nearly all the information that we have about the psychology of religion comes, therefore, from different kinds of questionnaires and interviews. Although those kinds of information allow fair comparisons of the answers that are given, some religious people believe that any systematic questions about their religious beliefs are impertinent, invasive or irrelevant. For many, religion is an area of life that is only brought out when they are troubled. For a few others, religion *is* their life.

Since conclusions about the believed truth or falsity of religious doctrines and their implications depend on what is said about them, every question must be worded carefully to ensure that the answers are unambiguous. Because the answers to questions about religion *are* convergent, we must conclude that no one has built their religion for themselves: but, given the opportunity, people will reveal their own constructions and misconceptions of the formal doctrines they have been offered, or have chosen. Any general assent to a set of doctrines must therefore be carefully distinguished from the personal meanings attributed to them, and from the errors or inconsistencies we are not aware of. To pool answers from the members of any group will establish broad trends, but it hides the uniqueness of particular replies.

Table 2 shows characteristic patterns of assent to a few typical religious questions, and emphasizes the similarity of beliefs among Christians as they follow broadly prescribed patterns of belief and behaviour. Our religious attitudes and attachments have developed within those accepted patterns, unless we are not religious, belong to some other tradition, or have given up conventional beliefs.

We must separate any explicit social influences from the subjective or individual reactions that make religious doctrines credible to us. When deeply-hidden mystical or ecstatic experiences and beliefs are described to another person they are, like our dreams, made to appear more coherent, rational or stereotyped than the primary experiences that are being described might have appeared to be at the time.

While sociologists of religion commonly report the percentages of responses in various socially important categories, like age, sex or denomination, and in doing so emphasize the levels of agreement with separate items, psychologists examine the internal coherence or the structure of responses from different groups across sets of separate measures. That procedure involves inter-correlating the scores for each measure to identify the patterns of relationship behind the variables.

Brown (1981) has reported two sets of results from a questionnaire that included both religious and broadly social, moral and political items which was answered by a group of people in Britain in 1950, and much later by an Australian group in 1978. A similar pattern of relationship among the religious measures emerged on both occasions, and identified a 'religionism' factor. This factor involves not only belief in God, in survival after death, and in the view that one cannot live a good life without religion, it also includes belief in the immorality of abortion and extra-marital sex and disapproval of complete freedom of speech. The second factor in those studies involved political beliefs and contrasts socialism with capitalism. Other studies (e.g., Francis 1985) have shown that this 'religionism' factor is also unrelated to measures of personality. Even when there is a positive relationship between religion and personality it is as likely that religion influences personality as it is that personality factors influence religion (cf. Spilka et al., 1985, pp. 310–12).

The structure of religion is rather like the structure of intelligence, which is measured by different tests of verbal and non-verbal or practical ability. As well as a concept of 'general intelligence' we easily recognize specific abilities that cover linguistic, arithmetic, spatial,

TABLE 2

Showing the affirmative answers (in percentages) from students at the University of New South Wales in 1986 to a set of religious questions (N = number of students questioned).

	Roman Catholics N = 120	Greek Orthodox N = 25	Anglican N = 50	Uniting Church N = 15	Lutheran N = 16	'No religion' N = 241
Do you believe there is a God?	90	88	82	87	69	37
Is there a life hereafter?	69	52	61	87	56	24
Did Christ perform miracles such as changing water into wine?	69	44	51	93	63	16
Do you go to church almost every week?	52	12	27	73	56	8
Do you pray several times a week?	48	28	42	53	63	12
Will there be a second coming of Christ?	45	36	39	80	63	12
Is there a Devil and a Hell in afterlife?	36	40	45	60	63	13
Do you feel sure there's only one true religion?	25	28	37	47	56	10
Are you very religious (more than most people)?	30	32	22	40	44	6
Is everything turning out just like the prophets of the Bible said it would?	15	16	33	40	44	6
Do you read the Bible several times a week?	7	8	20	47	50	3

mechanical and other skills. In a similar way, while we often identify some people as 'religious' because of their church-going, we can also identify them (as they might see themselves) by their membership of particular denomination, by their concern about what they should believe, by their religious observance or by their Christian experience and conversion. Arguments about the most important criteria of a religious orientation, and to what extent it depends on innate characteristics, the effects of training or the cultural environment, are still being debated. However, one very clear finding is that even among quite diverse groups of people responses to explicitly religious questions, or to questions with religious implications, are always coherent.

Measures of religion

It is important to remember that great care is needed in framing the items or questions that are to be the basis of any psychological or social study, since unclear or ambiguous questions do not yield interpretable results. If, for example, you want to know if people believe in a personal God, a loving God, a personally loving God, or in a personal and loving God, it is essential to ask those questions specifically, rather than hoping that people will draw these distinctions as they answer a vague inquiry. In a descriptive study of the religion of students in America in 1948 Gordon Allport asked them to 'check the one statement which most nearly expresses your belief'. His first alternative began: 'There is an infinitely wise, omnipotent Creator of the Universe and of natural laws, whose protection and favor may be supplicated through worship and prayer. God is a personal God.' The second of the seven alternatives was: 'There is an infinitely intelligent and friendly Being, working according to natural laws through which He expresses His power and goodness. There is the possibility of communication with this Deity in the sense that prayer may at least affect our moral attitude toward nature and toward our own place in the scheme of things.'

In a group of American students, 25 per cent of the men and 40 per cent of the women accepted Allport's first statement and 27 per cent of the men and 19 per cent of the women accepted the second, while 17 per cent of men and 12 per cent of women checked a later alternative: 'Because of our necessary ignorance in this matter, I neither believe nor disbelieve in a God.'

Like the others in Allport's list, these statements each contain components that can be agreed or disagreed with, since believing in an 'omnipotent creator' can be quite different from believing in a 'personal God'. The answers are therefore hard to interpret. Since Allport's time we have become more sophisticated about the need for clearly-worded statements, and about the way data can be analysed, although mistakes are still possible. An important choice must be made between asking open questions like, 'Which translation of the Bible do you prefer to read to yourself?' to which, in a recent study, only 5 per cent were able (or willing) to give a specific answer, and offering alternative answers to choose from. The question about preferred translations of the Bible could have been closed off by asking, 'Do you prefer to read the Authorised (King James) Version, the Good News Bible, or the New Jerusalem Bible?' But in that case, while the answers might seem plausible they could be invalid because one of the alternatives on offer can be ticked without the person questioned knowing anything about them. Every set of results depends on the quality of the questions that are asked, and while early psychologists almost invariably relied on spontaneous answers to direct questions for their data, not only is such material easily misinterpreted by the investigator, it is also hard to codify.

Another study of mine (Brown and Forgas, 1980) collected the ideas or concepts that people think are 'characteristic of religion and religious behaviour and belief'. This material was then reduced to a list of the most common features, and each of them was rated by another sample of people on a number of adjective scales which included active-passive, tense-relaxed and known-unknown. The analysis of these data, using a complex multi-dimensional scaling procedure, produced three separate factors. The first contrasted institutional and individual features of religion, the second involved positive or negative evaluations of religion, and the third distinguished what is tangible from what is intangible in religion, by setting 'church authority' against 'miracles' and 'church institutions' against 'salvation'. This study unpacked one set of the components of 'religionism'. We will see in Chapter Six that the other components that have been identified usually rely, not on what is informally understood by 'religion', but on what religions actually make available.

Other studies have asked people to rate and evaluate statements of attitudes or beliefs about religious issues, or to compare religious beliefs or prejudices directly (by asking, for example, 'Is a belief in Christ or in the Holy Spirit the more important?' or, 'Are Catholics more faithful than Protestants?'). Material gathered in this way draws on the consistent but implicit criteria by which religions are judged. Formal measurement scales have also been constructed to assess 'religious orthodoxy', 'attitudes to the Church' or prejudices about denominations by means of carefully selected items or statements.

One of the first scaling procedures was developed in 1929 by Thurstone and Chave, who measured attitudes to the Church by using

TABLE 3

Selected items from Thurstone and Chave's (1929) scale measuring attitude toward the Church. Scale values are in brackets, high scores being unfavourable to the Church.

Tick every statement below that expresses your sentiment toward the Church. Interpret the statements in accordance with your own experience with Churches.

10.	(10.5)	I regard the Church as a static, crystallized institution and as such it is unwholesome and detrimental to society and the individual.
21.	(9.5)	I think the Church is hundreds of years behind the times and cannot make a dent on modern life.
13.	(8.2)	The paternal and benevolent attitude of the Church is quite distasteful to me.
42.	(7.2)	I think the Church allows denominational differences to appear larger than true religion.
36.	(5.9)	The Churches may be doing good and useful work but they do not interest me.
9.	(4.7)	I am careless about religion and church relationships but I would not like to see my attitude become general.
16.	(3.9)	I believe the Church is fundamentally sound but some of its adherents have given it a bad name.
29.	(3.3)	I enjoy my church because there is a spirit of friendliness there.
45.	(2.2)	I like to go to church for I get something worth while to think about and it keeps my mind filled with right thoughts.
22.	(1.0)	I believe the Church has grown up with the primary purpose of perpetuating the spirit and teachings of Jesus and deserves loyal support.

the statements in Table 3, each of which has an empirically-derived attitude scale-value attached to it, based on the average of a large set of separate judgements about how favourable each of those statements is to religion. The measure of a person's attitude to religion is then calculated as the average scale-value of the statements that they have agreed with. Not only religion, but attitudes to beauty, size and to many other issues can be measured in this way.

A very large number of reasonably well-validated measures of religion are now available, and a good place to begin looking for them is in Robinson and Shaver's collection of *Measures of Social Psycho-*

logical Attitudes (1973), which has a section on measures of religion.

With a simple modification of Thurstone's scaling, Likert asked people to rate directly how much they agreed with each item in a set of carefully selected statements. He used a standard scale of agreement or belief and assigned scores to the answers from +3 or +2 (for strong agreement) through 0 (for neither agree or disagree) to −2 or −3 (for strong disagreement). A final score was found by adding up the values assigned to the step chosen for each alternative on that verbally identified scale. A Likert scale for the evaluation of religious beliefs (with the weights assigned) would be like this:

'I strongly agree that . . .' (score +2)
'I weakly agree that . . .' (+1)
'I am unsure whether I agree or disagree that . . .' (0)
'I weakly disagree that . . .' (−1)
'I strongly disagree that . . .' (−2)

A set of statements to which that scale can be applied is in Table 4.

TABLE 4

Martin and Westie's (1959) Fundamentalism Scale (using a Likert measurement procedure)

1. SA A U D SD	The Bible is the inspired word of God.
2. SA A U D SD	The religious idea of heaven is not much more than superstition.
3. SA A U D SD	Christ was a mortal, historical person, but not a supernatural or divine being.
4. SA A U D SD	Christ is a divine being, the Son of God.
5. SA A U D SD	The stories in the Bible about Christ healing sick and lame persons by his touch are fictitious and mythical.
6. SA A U D SD	Some day Christ will return.
7. SA A U D SD	The idea of life after death is simply a myth.
8. SA A U D SD	If more of the people in this country would turn to Christ we would have a lot less crime and corruption.
9. SA A U D SD	Since Christ brought the dead to life, he gave eternal life to all who have faith.

Note: Items 1, 4, 6, 8 and 9 are 'positive' for scoring purposes, and are added, while 2, 3, 5, and 7 are 'negative' items, and their scores are subtracted from the total.
SA = Strongly agree, scores +2,
A = Agree, scores +1,
U = Unsure, scores 0,
D = Disagree, scores −1,
SD = Strongly disagree, scores −2.

The ratings of the statements in Tables 3 and 4 disregard differences in the implicit meanings of these social or religious assertions. They are simply used as statements of attitudes, forms of belief, or stimuli for people to respond to. Fullerton and Hunsberger (1982) built a specifically doctrinal measure of Christian orthodoxy like this, deriving items from the creeds rather than following a diffuse, even if socially recognized, form of religion. Their items include, 'Christ is a divine being, the Son of God', 'Some day Christ will return', 'The idea of life after death is simply a myth', 'If more of the people in this country would turn to Christ we would have a lot less crime and corruption', 'Since Christ brought the dead to life, He gave eternal life to all who have faith.' These statements are not designed to be tricky or to trip people up but they try to capture and draw agreement or disagreement in the terms that people might use to express themselves. They are, therefore, standardized in the same sense that the Church's creeds are authoritative statements that provide a point of reference for Christian belief.

The 'Shepherd Scale' (Bassett et al., 1981) was developed to assess fundamentalism, using biblical texts as stimuli, as in the item: 'I believe that God raised Jesus from the dead (John 20.24–29; 1 Corinthians 15.3–8)'. It is, however, unusual for explicit doctrines or texts to maintain a person's religious position beyond whatever might be implied by, for example, ratifying the baptismal promise which asks, 'Do you believe in God, the Father Almighty, maker of heaven and earth?', with the prescribed response 'I do'; and later asserting 'All this I firmly believe' in answer to the question: 'And do you believe in the Holy Spirit; the holy Catholic Church; the communion of saints; the forgiveness of sins; the resurrection of the body, and the life everlasting?' But doctrines like these have divided religious traditions from one another, as the *filioque* clause in the Nicene Creed, which identifies the Spirit proceeding from the Son, has divided the Eastern from the Western Churches since the twelfth century.

Since people can sensibly answer only one question at a time there are important differences between catechetical, psychological, and other forms of interrogation. Although a knowledge-based investigation might expect correct answers to questions about, say, the authorship of the Acts of the Apostles, statements of attitudes or belief only have a 'correct' answer if they correspond to an ideologically defined position, such as 'Religion is the opium of the people'. Yet all who would agree that 'Jesus rose on the third day' are unlikely to give the same meaning to that statement, because it can be interpreted literally, metaphorically or symbolically. Religious knowledge is, in this mode, intangible, while the boundaries and context of meaning can shift. Whenever knowledge is closely linked to faith (and to belief), confidence in it can be shattered or displaced, although, as we have seen (p. 11 above), people are in general less confident about the truth or falsity of verifiable propositions, such as whether or not there are tigers in China, than they are about strictly religious propositions.

Studies of knowledge-based measures of religion, as in the work of Glock and Stark (1965), have shown that very few people can name the books in the Bible (which most people might not regard as an important piece of information). But very few people are well-informed about political issues or know the name of their local Member of Parliament or the policies of each party. Such 'general (trivial?) knowledge' has been shown to be independent of the confidence that is placed in either a religious or political system. It could be for this reason that 'religious education', as opposed to a 'theological training', emphasizes moral principles, how to behave at church, and what 'being religious' might do for you.

Some other procedures

The methods we have mentioned so far all involve a direct approach to what people will say about themselves, and this is often tailored to convey socially 'desirable' information. For that reason various indirect measures have been developed in which what the subject is asked to regard as the primary task conceals the investigator's main interest. Projective tests are the best known of these, in which people may be asked to tell a story about an ambiguous picture of, for example, someone at prayer, in order to establish whether religious ideas are unwittingly introduced. These methods have been used extensively to study the developing understanding of children, but they are less favoured now than they were about twenty years ago, largely because there is no adequate way to validate whatever conclusions might be reached. They have also been dismissed as too subjective, because they depend so much on the judgement of the person who interprets the results.

An indirect procedure that *is* objective relies on measures of physiological response (or arousal), such as changes in differential skin temperature while subjects are responding to religious or to other stimuli. Those methods have not, however, given useful (or consistent) results, primarily because our most informative religious responses are closely tied to the language which carries meanings and explanations. Furthermore, not only can physiological responses not distinguish between positive and negative evaluations, but our feelings of confidence or security as we listen to or sing familiar prayers or hymns are too complex to be measured as microscopic physiological responses.

Controlled observations

Having decided exactly what to study, the important decisions an investigator has to make concern whether to experiment or simply to observe and describe, whether to let the subjects control what is said or to offer closed categories into which their responses must be put. We must also decide whether to look only at people who are already religious (however that is identified) or to look more broadly at the reactions to religion that are embedded (and even isolated) within a total social or cultural context.

It is now accepted that when religion is studied from the outside and compared against other social processes the religionism factor we have mentioned (which some have identified with 'religiosity') is found; when religion is looked at from the inside, separate aspects of it are found. As in the rest of science our findings depend on the level of abstraction of any study, on what is being looked for, and on the methods that are used to gather the data. The conclusions that are reached are therefore cumulative, although many church people seem to think that every study in the psychology or sociology of religion must start from the beginning, by asking the same old questions afresh. They neglect the extent to which most of these problems have already been looked at by others, and that the earlier findings will be buried somewhere in the social science literature. The best investigations are not set up inductively, as is so commonly assumed (although that is the way new problems must be approached). Really good studies are designed to test specific hypotheses, unless the aim is simply to describe or count those who are either for or against on some issue.

The search for 'facts' about church members often implies a marketing strategy to find who else is similar to them and might be attracted into the membership. It is necessary to be sure, however, that you can *reliably* or accurately count whatever characteristics are important, and that you will be able to make valid interpretations of any data. Most of our initial inferences about others' intentions and philosophies of life are almost inevitably mistaken because of our tendency to jump to easy conclusions. To find what people 'really' believe we must listen carefully, and not guide the conversation or ask too many questions that can throw the other person off the track. Our questions themselves often indicate what we think the 'right' answer should be. Confidential disclosures are usually made only to those who deserve a personal view, and questioners are easily 'taken in' when they forget that strangers are seldom given privileged information.

The 'sample survey' methods inevitably elicit information that is publicly acceptable or will convey a particular point of view. The ambiguity of most things we say and the ways we can cover up any unorthodox but religiously committed attitudes that could draw on strong prejudices, means that our conclusions about other people tend to align whatever religious characteristics they display with other information about them. So W. H. Clark (1958, p. 209) asserted that the members of 'sacramental churches' differ from those who accept a 'sterner theology', and that Catholicism produces 'less anxiety because of confession, the sacraments and such like'. But he had little evidence, apart from his own judgement, for those assertions. Pratt (1920) similarly argued that Catholics and Protestants must have a different temperament, because he believed that the worship of Catholics is 'objective' and that Protestant worship is 'subjective'. It is a general finding, however, that while observers attribute personality-based consistencies to other people, they are themselves confident that their actions and decisions are well-reasoned and tuned to the demands of particular situations. The effect of this difference in perspective and interpretation is known as the 'fundamental attribution error'.

Religious experiments

Experimental procedures set up well-controlled conditions within which observations can be made. The most notorious experiment from recent studies of religion involved a comparison of the mystical experiences that might be induced by non-prescription drugs or by listening to a Good Friday service. Although that original study was carried out less than twenty-five years ago (Pahnke, 1966), scientific work is far more constrained now than it was then, and it would be impossible to replicate it because of the greater ethical control there is today over all experimental work. People have also become 'immunized' against psychological experiments. Furthermore, some religious people believe that to control the conditions for any observations of God's action is irreconcilable with that action itself or with our independent responsiveness.

In Pahnke's famous experiment, one Good Friday at Harvard University twenty Christian theological students listened over loud-speakers in the chapel to a two-and-a-half-hours religious service. Half of them had been given psilocybin an hour-and-a-half earlier; the other matched half had been given an inert drug as a placebo control.

Neither the subjects nor the experimenters knew who was in which group. The dependent measures that were collected at various times up to six months later involved scaled ratings of their experiences and tape-recorded accounts of their feelings. Pahnke found, using accepted statistical procedures, that those in the experimental or drug condition reported significantly more positive religious experiences than did the non-drug controls who only listened to the service.

This experiment emphasizes that although we might disapprove of what any experiment aims to bring under control, they do allow firm conclusions to be made about the effects that are operating in controlled conditions. Scientific experiments and systematic observations are not new to the psychology of religion. In 1870 Francis Galton (1883) found no effects of religion on the longevity of Catholics, Protestants, Jews and agnostics. Galton also noted that the kin of prayerful people did not recover from illness more rapidly than did the kin of the 'unprayerful', and that members of Royal Houses, whose longevity is regularly prayed for, did not live longer than ordinary people. Although such comparisons can be rejected as an unfair test of the efficacy of prayer, they show that it is possible to evaluate the challenges to religious truth that are often made.

Another widely-cited experiment is described by Darley and Batson (1973), who watched to see if seminary students who had, or had not, just read the parable of the Good Samaritan acted differently when they came across someone in apparent distress. In that experiment, groups of theological students were asked to help with a piece of research. When they agreed, each person was asked to go to another office to complete the study. Some were told to hurry, and others were not; some had read the Good Samaritan story, others had not. Along the way they all passed a confederate of the experimenter who was sitting uneasily in an alley, playing the role of an incapacitated person. The dependent measure in that experiment simply concerned the differences between those who did or did not stop to offer help. It was found that those who had not been told to hurry were most likely to stop. Whether they had or had not recently read the story of the Good Samaritan had no effect on the likelihood that they would help.

Many church members are aware that when changes are introduced to the liturgy, the times of services, or even to the operation of the Sunday-school, they are often justified as an 'experiment', not because the effects would be evaluated systematically but as a convenient way to explain their tentativeness. If those 'experiments' were to be properly evaluated they could, however, help make decisions for change that would not just be based on intuition. Scientists must be as conscientious about setting up their experiments correctly as religious people are in getting their religion right, as they satisfy the conditions for a valid sacrament or for keeping the congregation alive.

It is widely agreed that there are few true experiments in the psychology of religion (cf. Deconchy, 1985, 1987). Although many studies have been analysed *as if* they were well-controlled 'experiments', when the major variable involves religion itself the subjects can never be *randomly* assigned to separate religious and non-religious treatment conditions because they belong to one of those categories anyway. The constraints from both practical *and* ethical considerations therefore force us to get as close as we can to the ideal experiment with quasi-experiments that analyse data by comparing the responses from known or separately identified groups that can be expected to show differences. Deconchy discusses a number of quasi-experiments in religion that have considered the effects of non-verbal signs (including forms of dress and wearing a clerical collar), reminders of death, and of anonymity itself on the way religious attitudes are expressed to others, as well as the effects of peer pressures and religious or lay investigators on the results that are obtained. In all of these experiments, religious contexts have been found to have a considerable effect on what is expressed.

Beyond comparative studies of religious and non-religious people, it has been shown that religious groups that have severe forms of initiation have a more coherent membership than those which it is easy to enter. This simple example emphasizes that religious and other institutions influence the beliefs, identity and goals of their members.

Summary

Before quantified methods were developed that could be applied to the study of religion, casual descriptions of feelings, beliefs, or knowledge formed the data that were used to support rather informal arguments about it, except when the numbers of those who could be expected to support a cause were directly counted. It is now very common to use carefully worded questionnaires and some experimental control to sharpen expected differences between specified groups, and also to manipulate the conditions under which data are gathered. Any study relies on the co-operation of quite large numbers of people to establish reliable trends, which necessarily cancel out idiosyncratic responses or errors in the data.

Wittgenstein remarked that we would feel intellectually distant from someone who claimed to have been on the moon but could not say how that might have happened. So it is with Christians. They are expected to know about their faith and their claims for it are expected to be consistent with the norms of some religious group, and to satisfy other (usually informal) tests of credibility which might refer to texts, traditions and the authorities that support their personal experience and beliefs. It is also important to know when it is better to keep quiet about one's religion. None of these features of religion is easy to measure, and we have to be beware of prosaic or conventional perspectives that get trapped by social pressures. There is no independent knowledge of reality beyond our shared experiences and what we have been told or can reason through.

An essential feature of psychological data is the way they externalize, or make mental processes accessible to study. The simplest questions about religion ask: 'How often do you go to church?', 'What does religion mean to you?' and 'Have you ever had an experience of the divine?' Because such questions are open-ended, those answering them can decide what they will say and how much detail to give. This makes it hard to compare answers without assuming co-operation or without reading additional meanings into what is said. Asking people to select one answer from among a list of alternatives gives more reliable, if simpler and less valid, data since it is too easy to claim belief in what is not understood. (This is so despite William James's assertion that a person is unlikely to say he believes something he does not imagine that he understands. James therefore argued for a distinction between reactions to the elements of a proposition, and 'the psychic attitude to the proposition as a whole' (1889, p. 325).)

Before searching for deeply hidden meanings behind any religious attitudes we have to resolve many simple questions about religion, including those about the way religious people differ from those who are not religious, and the effects of religiousness on a person's behaviour and attitudes. An important change in our everyday curiosity about religious people has been produced by a scientific interest that, in testing theories, asks those same questions but with more stringent standards of evidence. And no religious inquiry is theologically (or morally) neutral, whether it supports an argument, gauges opinion or evaluates a church-based programme. But to say that you are 'doing a survey' has become an acceptable excuse for visiting strangers, making contact with those who may have lapsed, raising awareness about current issues, or simply for exploring and perhaps changing attitudes.

A Maori proverb says that one can see the corners of a house, but not of the heart. The causal networks in a scientific analysis may have a similar superficiality compared with an existential confidence in religion that is not exposed but contains deeply personal meanings. It is easier to calibrate assent to a religion than to capture those deep convictions. Our social norms favour expressions of religion that do not appear to be too strongly committed, except among religious professionals and those who themselves help to control and identify the content of a religion through hymns, extempore prayers and conversation. The best information will, however, open new ways to study religion, and balance theory with practice.

4 Religious Behaviour and Observance

To think that a rain-making ritual is primarily a technique (or magic) for producing rain is to project nineteenth century utilitarianism onto the primitive mind.

Suzanne Langer

My own view is that savage religion is something not so much thought out as danced out.

R. R. Marett (1914)

An incorrigible dualism in western thought has led Christians to subdue the body through ascetic and penitential practices, extolling the mind for its intellectual and other commitments, expecting weakness when faced with immediate demands from, and the need to service, the body. But it is not just for theoretical reasons that mental and physical processes, or mind and body, have been separated. They are differently represented in our experience, and we rely on mental processes to control and escape from the bodily self in meditation, prayer and fasting. At the same time Christians 'look for the resurrection of the body', in whatever way that doctrine is understood. Hindus and Buddhists anticipate reincarnation in another form that will reward their moral success, or punish their failure, in this life.

While direct sensory stimulation by 'bells and smells' and by music is common in worship, to bring the mind 'closer to God', it is also a familiar source of comfort. Yet there is continuing controversy about this, and many Protestants set their simpler forms of worship against the use of vestments, incense and processions in Catholic services. William Sargant wrote in his *Battle for the Mind* (1957, p. 107): 'Voodoo dances, drums, and other methods producing feelings (*sic*) of conversion to, and possession by, gods, can alone cause such states of brain excitement (as extreme inhibition and emotional exhaustion) in suitable subjects.' That is a cautious statement when it is read carefully; yet it has encouraged some people to argue for the primacy of physiological processes, not only in the 'brain-washing' or 'thought-reform' that is assumed to characterize belief changes manipulated by authoritarian political regimes but in religious conversions as well. Those methods of control are assumed to be 'emotional' rather than rational. They are therefore not highly valued, and imply a theory of behaviour-change that emphasizes the

44

effects of explicit pressure by others, rather than an individual's own choice.

Other cultures or groups do not foster the same beliefs about these processes. In modern China, for example, mind has been taken to be a reflection of external social reality, so that our western philosophical idealism was criticized from a materialist perspective and 're-education' and written confessions were used during the Cultural Revolution to correct bourgeois thinking and similarly 'false' ideas. The Catholic Church has also been criticized for using direct methods of social control. William Sargant wrote that:

> The leaders of successful faiths have never dispensed entirely with physiological weapons (and bodily control) in their attempts to confer spiritual grace on their fellow men. Fasting, chastening of the flesh by scourging and physical discomfort, regulation of breathing, disclosure of awesome mysteries, drumming, dancing, singing, inducement of panic, fear, weird or glorious lighting, incense, intoxicant drugs and these are only some of the many methods used to modify normal brain functioning for religious purposes (p. 73).

Religious behaviour, which is undoubtedly complex and can be found within or outside religious contexts, is not necessarily enforced by social influence or control. It has both public and private components, the latter involving intentions that may or may not be socially approved. For that reason, learning how to be religious or show religiousness in public is an important but neglected feature of religious training, formation or socialization. One needs only watch tourists on their visits to churches, especially if they arrive while a service is in progress, to realize the unfamiliarity of many people with what is accepted and expected in church. Psychologists refer to such knowledge as the competence which underlies particular 'perform-ances', which are themselves governed by more or less well-defined social rules. We noted in Chapter Two that some of those rules are formally prescribed in the rubrics, while others are set by convention, with an ill-defined tolerance of what is allowable, like when to pray or sing, whom to proselytize, when to march in the streets or invoke religious sanctions for action.

F. H. Allport's (1934) results given in Figure 5 (p. 27) stress the consistency of explicit behaviour, and the place of simple conformity, rather than whatever is to be regarded as the 'deeply' psychological reasons for actions. Apparent piety is therefore not a good guide to religiousness, since it can be quite superficial. If religious people are to be known by their 'fruits', these are necessarily ambiguous. Actions like going to church, giving money or time, may involve social conformity and secret reservations. Although what we *do* becomes public, it does not necessarily imply a strong religious commitment. But what are the effects of religion if we assume that a commitment to it is to some (unknown) extent public and in some sense covert? The effects of religion on social prejudice, sexual behaviour, political preferences and voting patterns can involve direct control or they might reflect non-religious attitudes and other tendencies to act in particular ways. Furthermore, the attitudes expressed do not necessarily imply a willingness to act, but can be used to support, justify or change the meaning of action. So, for example, someone who says they are 'religious' does not necessarily go to church, and we can deduce little about the doctrines or practices that a person accepts simply from knowing that they attend church regularly. Nevertheless, what is said or done must have some social sanction if one is not to risk being identified as irrational.

Church membership

While little can be concluded about the religious orientation or strength of attachment of someone who says she 'goes to church weekly', we gain confidence if we know that such a person also receives communion, takes regular religious instruction, reads the Bible, prays before meals or before bed, thinks about moral rules in religious terms, and regards herself as a good representative of her faith. Some of those conclusions can be reached by watching what religious people do, but it is easier (and quicker) to ask them about their religious behaviour and attitudes, only making direct observations about things they are unlikely to be aware of, like whom they talk to in mixed race or denominational groups, or who they sit near in church. The results of such studies show, however, that the members of religious groups act like those in any other group, since they all observe the same broad social rules about how to act in specific situations, whether or not that involves what are strictly defined as 'religious' actions. Small congregations have therefore been found to be friendlier than large ones, simply because social interaction is easier there. A specifically religious perspective is only needed to explain a few social phenomena.

Among some explicitly committed religious (or anti-religious) people, the overtly religious characteristics of dress, diet or forms of address extend their religion into broader social domains, thereby identifying or marking them off. It is the same with explanations of

behaviour. While John Wesley, for example, attributed the conversions he observed to the intervention of the Holy Ghost, others have
accounted for them with reference to a breakdown (or reconstruction)
of belief under stress, or to a constitutional predisposition to persuasion. Because we can only display our intentions by what we say or do,
others must draw their conclusions about our character, personality or
temperament from that information. So people in clerical dress, for
example, constrain what will be said to them (James Joyce's Bloom
crossed the road when he saw a group of nuns coming towards him).
But what people do that is 'religious' (or has a religious intention),
although obvious to some, does not necessarily convey any information about the person, since so much of anyone's religion is shared and
prescribed, being bound to language and what people are ready to say
about it. Because of that, when the Churches publish statistics about
the numbers of churches and clergy, the numbers of communicants,
communions, baptisms, and so on, they are giving information about
their social acceptance and support. This has an institutional focus.
While religious people will be involved there, more information is
needed to establish who they are, their characteristics and whether
they accept the demands expected of them. The discrepancy between
what is prescribed and what is actually done has encouraged psychologists and others to identify forms of the attachment or the distance
that individuals set between their own actions and the demands of an
institutional religion in terms of hypocrisy or commitment.

To visit a Hindu or Buddhist temple emphasizes how hard it might
be to understand or accept what another's religion involves. Despite
that, we can easily classify both Christian and non-Christian traditions
for their social distance from each other or their similarity to our own
perspective. Prejudice and false information often clouds our
attempts to 'understand' what any others' practices entail, and how
they might differ from or be like our own. That religions are so heavily
loaded with the culturally specific meanings and experience of a
particular tradition may explain why so many religious people stay in
the traditions they have grown up with. It has been found that few
people defect from their religious tradition if their parents maintained
an active involvement with it at least until they (their children) had
moved away from home (see also p. 101, below). Those who leave
home do not automatically align themselves with another church
group, partly because they may find it hard to establish new social
bonds there. Religious (and other) groups therefore appear closed, to
their outsiders. That community or diffuse attachments to religion
and not the erosion of traditional beliefs or a loss of identity as a church
member account for changes in the norms about accepted religious

behaviour is shown by the extent to which the numbers accepting traditional religious beliefs have dropped more slowly than has church attendance itself (cf. Mol, 1985).

Church attendance

While it is still important for some people to go to church, especially at Easter and Christmas, more frequent church attenders tend to be aligned with a conservative political stance, and religious denominations are themselves ranked along a conservative-liberal dimension. Although adults with young children appear to be the most frequent church attenders, one probably gets closer to the heart of a religion by regularly going to church than by reading theological manuals or prayer books.

It is a long way from analyses of what a religion formally requires to a knowledge of the implications of any indicators of religion, whether in church membership or institutional involvement. Gallup Poll data, for example, show that in the United States 98 per cent of households have a Bible, 94 per cent of adults there believe in God, 82 per cent claim a 'religious' or denominational 'preference', 69 per cent claim to be church members, 57 per cent say religious beliefs are important to them, and 41 per cent go to church weekly. In Australia, a 1981 Gallup survey found that 12 per cent of Anglicans, 34 per cent of those who belonged to the Uniting Church and 37 per cent of Roman Catholics said they had been to church in the last seven days. Furthermore, those who go to church at least once a week are more similar in religious terms to equally regular attenders in other denominations, than they are to infrequent church attenders in their own denomination. Yet there are still prejudices against too-frequent attendance. Frequent Mass attendance among Catholics, for example, is sometimes attributed to the power and control of the priests. There is also consistent evidence that women in all denominations attend church more frequently than men. A Morgan Gallup Poll in Australia in 1981 found that 26 per cent of women and 18 per cent of men said they had attended church during the previous week, and that 40 per cent of Catholic women and 30 per cent of Catholic men said they had been to church in the last month. This finding may not relate simply to gender, since the recent Australian Values Study showed that of the women who said they had attended church in the last month, 18 per cent were in full-time work, 35 per cent were in part-time work and 33 per cent (compared with 23 per cent of the men) were not in the work force.

Social surveys have shown that church attendance is related to occupation, education and age, but while church attendance is the best measure of involvement with a religious institution, it is not independent of gender and higher socio-economic status. Such effects can be explained with reference to the nature or conventions of church life, and the activities that are offered, which may discourage those who are not socially at ease with other people and who do not enjoy, or who find it hard to share, activities with those who are. This has always been a problem the Churches must deal with, and it is clear that in the United States at least, those of lower social status have less involvement not only with the church, but with social clubs, community service groups, political parties and parent–teacher associations. This selective process defines one of the boundaries that must be overcome by those who believe that church attendance is an essential sign of religiousness.

While it is commonly assumed that actual church-going has declined, the significance of this is debatable. Some moralists and clergy look no further than the bare figures. But this change interacts with other social trends, including reduced demands imposed on church members (such as the old custom of fasting before communion) and competing activities. Perhaps the higher levels of church-going in the past simply reflected a customary conformity. It is therefore unclear whether lower church attendance reflects a move towards an alienation from religion, mere abstention or the substitution of religious beliefs and activities by something else.

Contemporary society is not like that of our fathers and grandfathers, who were less well-educated than their children, had a shorter life and rather different values. Secularization provides an easy explanation of this phenomenon, since religious control over the public domain has been reduced by increased state involvement in education, health and welfare, and the ubiquitous news media vigorously acquaint us with competing systems of meaning that might claim allegiance, like sport, politics, tourism and new 'adult toys'. Whether as a result of industrialization or a true ideological change, social life is no longer built around the daily office, the Church's year and the cycles of baptism, confirmation, marriage, prayers for the sick, burial of the dead and consolation of the bereaved except among religious professionals, those in crisis, and perhaps in rural areas where the pressures for social change are weaker and continuity or cohesion is greater.

Religious support

The British Values Study used the following indicators to measure attachments to institutional religion: 'the Church answers spiritual needs' (accepted by 42 per cent), it 'answers family problems' (32 per cent), 'answers moral problems' (30 per cent), 'there is one true religion' (21 per cent) and that 'one can have great confidence in the Church' (19 per cent). It is hard to know what to conclude from these data, except that the support for religion remains ahead of politics, art, sports and leisure. Even if being 'religious' means more than just going to church, religion is easily lost in its social context whenever the demands are readily accepted and satisfied. The classical differences between church and sect centre on their demands and forms of social integration, sects being more pressing, strident and socially exclusive (see also p. 65, below). They also resolve theological questions more convergently. Unlike arguments about the causes of conversion and what elicits a worshipful attitude, which could be settled by data from church people, theological debates focus on the traditional support that ought to be claimed for particular points of view.

Among the theories that would explain church-going we can find reference to habit, the appeal of strictness itself, compensation for social or personal deprivation, the rewards from the status that church membership carries, the social support and contact that is available there, and the opportunities given by church-going to express religious beliefs. Each of those explanations can be supported by *some* data, and we must conclude that church-going is neither the simple nor merely compensatory action that common prejudices often find it to be.

Summary

It is hard for psychologists to confine their attention to religious behaviour itself, since without further study it is uninformative and necessarily ambiguous. It is not helpful to know that bishops are on average two inches taller than their clergy, or that those who go to church daily are more religious than those who go either three times a year or less often, except for someone who is naively impressed by the 'facts'. Such differences do not mean that one group of religious people is necessarily 'better' than another. The implicit reasons for any social conformity, the consequences of formal alignments with religious institutions and the personal satisfaction of church-going must also be considered. The reasons for going to church could be simply social and not 'deeply' psychological. But in what ways are religiously active people different from those who are not so active? Crandall and Gozali (1969) showed that one important effect of a religious training was to make children more skilled at giving socially desirable replies. At another extreme, church-goers seem to be different from non-church-goers in their social characteristics. While church statistics about attendance can support administrative decisions concerning the use of buildings and staff, they tell us nothing about individual members, whose church attendance could involve either mere conformity to social rules or a thorough-going commitment to their faith.

5 Religion and Personality

Blessed are the poor in spirit: for theirs is the kingdom of heaven. Blessed are those who mourn . . . the meek . . . those who hunger and thirst for righteousness . . . the merciful . . . the pure in heart . . . the peacemakers . . . those who are persecuted for righteousness' sake . . . Blessed are you when men revile you and persecute you, and utter all kinds of evil against you falsely on my account.

Matthew 5.3–11

Perhaps it is because Christianity offers so many models of an ideal life in its saints and martyrs and because religion is expected to have some effect on its adherents that the personality characteristics of religious people has been the most commonly explored issue in both the psychology and sociology of religion. These studies have investigated acceptance of the Protestant work ethic, achievement motivation, educational or financial success, intelligence and creativity, authoritarianism and dogmatism, suggestibility and aggression, among religious and non-religious people (cf. Argyle and Beit-Hallahmi, 1975). But Bergin (1983) has failed to find much support for the view that any forms of religious belief and behaviour are directly related to personality traits (cf., p. 60 below). Inventories that would measure personality traits used to assume that the primary determinants of our individual differences are internal, involving a deliberate and conscious sense of self as well as some 'unconscious' or dynamic processes. Recent personality theories have, however, placed greater emphasis on the traits or characteristics that are assigned to us by other people, and on the ways we are constrained by our awareness of what social situations or contexts require or allow us to do. Other social constraints limit what we can properly disclose about ourselves and about our own inner life. That filtering process has an especially important effect on how we deal with our religion. Many people are defensive about their beliefs for fear that they will be misunderstood or criticized for them. While 18,000 or more English adjectives could be used to describe other people, only a few of them are widely used. They include 'religious', 'scientific' and 'artistic', since what we seem to like *doing* is assumed to reflect the kind of person we *are*. But to describe someone as 'religious' is very imprecise, and can be easily said without firm evidence about church-going, prayer or religious belief to support it.

The very great number of measures of personality available include scales to assess neuroticism and extraversion, which Francis (1985) has shown are not related to the strength of religious belief, as well as traits like openness or dogmatism, agreeableness or conscientiousness. Many of these measures include questions that refer directly to religious belief or practice, asking for example whether one accepts that 'Christ performed miracles such as changing water into wine', if one feels one is 'a special agent of God' or 'reads the Bible several times a week'. Those items from the Minnesota Multiphasic Personality Inventory (MMPI), which is the most widely used American personality inventory, simply assume that religion is an important facet of life, or of personality defined as the characteristics of individuals or people in general that account for consistent patterns of response to others and to the demands that social situations impose on them. Furthermore, when people are asked to say 'who' they are, they very frequently identify themselves in terms of their name, sex, occupation *and* religious denomination. The few consistent personality differences that have been found in the orientations of 'religious' and 'non-religious' people, and especially in their dogmatism, can be easily explained with reference to the effects of religious teaching, or to other aspects of their education and the consequences of status differences between religious groups (like Catholics and Protestants), without reference to any deeply personal characteristics or innate differences.

It is likely that reduced prejudice against particular religious groups and the recent conciliatory changes in doctrine and practice may have eliminated much of the tension between these groups, which generated expectations about differences between religious and other people. While it is *possible* that religious denominations do have specific effects on their members or recruit different types of people, there is little independent evidence of any strong differences, except for whatever is attributed to those who belong to specific groups. Knowing that someone is an 'evangelical' or an 'Anglo-Catholic' itself carries a halo of other characteristics linked with those labels.

Many personality characteristics are therefore to be found in the eyes of the beholders, and embedded in the words they use to describe other people. So it has been found that whether real people or stereotyped descriptions, like a 'suburban housewife' or an 'army general', are being rated, they produce similar personality factors (Mulaik, 1964). This work suggests that personality traits depend more on the words used or the roles assigned than on actual 'personality' characteristics. The personality differences assigned to religious groups or to their members are therefore confounded by the identified and stereotyped characteristics which we assign to 'religious people'.

It is not surprising, since a person's religion is expected to have some effect on them, that religious people are thought to be either suggestible or convergent, simply because they share many beliefs. In the same way, religions have been criticized for enforcing a passive compliance with their tenets, neglecting the different ways their adherents make sense of their doctrines and religious attachments. That such uniformity is no longer strongly enforced in the Church of England is shown in the recent Doctrine Commission's report, *We believe in God* (1987). While some will have absolute confidence in the truth of their religion and will try to live up to its standards, others are acutely aware of their failure to do so. And while religious people might be expected to be narrow-minded, self-centred and immune to the validity of others' disbelief, many of them try to maintain an open-minded search for 'the way, the truth and the life'. Those who fall short of a religious ideal do not necessarily criticize themselves for that. Although some people resolve the tension between secular and religious pressures by withdrawing to the religious life, others make some other sacrifice, are only religious 'on Sundays', or give it up altogether. Simplified interpretations of those separate solutions place God either inside or outside each of us, or lead us to expect a response that forces into 'outer darkness' those who reject any vision of God's people. This is itself partly a matter of the rhetoric that is used to describe those who might be 'religious'.

Religious values

Our goals, and the means we use to achieve whatever we value, lie half-way between personality processes and social attitudes. Milton Rokeach (1973, p. 111) found that students who said they valued religion as 'extremely important' in their everyday life were significantly different from those who said it was 'extremely unimportant' in terms of how they rated 'a comfortable life' (with religious people scoring it low), a 'sense of accomplishment' (high), 'family security' (high), 'pleasure' (low), 'salvation' (high), 'social recognition' (low), and whether they said they were themselves ambitious (with religious people scoring low), capable (low), forgiving (scoring high), helpful (high), honest (high), independent (low), intellectual (low), logical (low) and loving (high). While such values and attitudes are linked to our personality functioning, they are not exactly what the term 'personality' implies in its common use. Those who believe that religion is closely linked with psychological characteristics can therefore only expect to find consistent differences in social factors like age, sex and a broadly social conservatism.

We can conclude from this that since being 'religious' is socially constrained, religious people may show tender-minded, sympathetic and conservative attitudes more readily than they adopt a tough-minded or radical stance. The ways people express themselves religiously also depend on what is allowed or has to be done in specific situations, and on their familiarity with the areas of life that religion is related to. While those who are tough-minded conservatives are more likely to believe that women are inferior to men and that children should be punished to make them strong, tough-minded liberals tend to accept trial marriage and tender-minded conservatives tend to believe in the survival of death, and tender-minded liberals tend to accept pacifism. It is not clear how those preferences are related to other demands or to the norms of Christian groups that either allow gambling or reject it as sinful, or which identify marriage as primarily for love and companionship or as a 'remedy against sin . . .' (as the Book of Common Prayer has it). It could even be that it is the rules of religious *groups* that carry and express any personality differences attributed to their members.

Each person finds their own solution to whatever social and ideological constraints they accept. While therapists and confessors, friends, or others who try to help those who are distressed or fail to recognize the errors of their ways usually advocate solutions that have been accepted by other people, we all differ in the way we build an identity for ourselves within the habitual responses that others usually rely on to predict how we will act in specific situations.

And just as we gloss a text for clues about its author, and often fail to get that right because of our own biased interpretations, we expect to understand other people by analysing how they present themselves to us. But our success depends in part on our interaction with them. Unless 'religiousness' is taken as a stable biological or temperamental trait, like our own readiness to be roused to anger, fear, anxiety or sexuality, we are always constrained by situational demands and pressures. The way we acknowledge that reflects our upbringing and experience in a particular tradition, which also influences how we put it all together.

Family influences

In an Australian study among university students who had, or had not given up their religion, Hunsberger and Brown (1984) found that those for whom religion had been emphasized during their childhood, especially by their mother, were the most likely to have maintained an attachment with it. On the other hand those who had given religion up had been influenced by 'intellectual discussions' and by arguments about religious issues with their parents. The acceptance of religion by those who have been trained into it can therefore account for the fact that frequent church attendance, knowledge of religion and strength of religious belief are all highly correlated with a religious training in childhood, in which attending church schools can play either a positive or negative role (cf. Greeley, McCready and McCovat, 1976).

But few people are simply consumers or reproducers of whatever training they have been given. Just as we try to make sense of other people, we also make sense of our own experiences and develop a set of beliefs for ourselves. Whether we take these beliefs to be literally or metaphorically true and emphasize the fatherhood or the creative powers of God, the gifts of the Spirit rather than the resurrection, the control of religion or its liberating potential, seems to depend more strongly on our training, experiences and values than on the motivational traits that are commonly assumed to underlie personality processes. We must not, however, disregard the extent to which the religiousness of some people has become a part of their personality, influencing the kind of person they are.

Religious orientations

Separate religious orientations that have been identified contrast a sense of the nearness to God with a lack of confidence in his presence, and rely on individual or institutional sanctions, on experience of the divine or on a sense of routine obligation, humanistic or authoritarian emphases, and devotionalism or doctrinal orthodoxy. The most widely accepted contrast that psychologists use was advanced by Gordon Allport (1966), who distinguished an intrinsic, committed or goal-oriented attitude to religion from its extrinsic, consensual and means-oriented forms. Since none of those terms is neutral, we are likely to disapprove of one or the other response-set as a way to be religious, or to recognize other forms. So Daniel Batson has recently added a 'quest orientation', following Paul Tillich who said that 'all true religion is a path out of the quicksands of self-preoccupation and self-worship' (1957, p. 4).

The concern for a self-serving religiosity is captured in Allport's extrinsic orientation to religion which emphasizes doctrines that offer safety, social standing and solace, and endorse one's chosen way of life. When he said that an intrinsic orientation 'regards faith as a supreme value in its own right . . . oriented to a unification of being that takes seriously the commandment of brotherhood and strives to transcend all self-centered needs' (1966), Allport recognized the open-ended and creative religious attachment that is quite different from a religion of control which promises some final reward for our good behaviour now. That is probably the most commonly encountered form of religion, and one that is easily rejected, not least when it conflicts with the openness and independence encouraged by other social and educational models or practice.

That some people will accept a religious position without question could either reflect social sanctions or the closed-minded and instrumental attitude that reflects the social prejudices that Rokeach (1960) identified at the root of a dogmatic personality. Dogmatism seems to be associated with membership of hierarchically organized groups (such as the Catholic Church), a general intolerance or authoritarianism, and the belief that an outside authority is able to resolve one's fears of loneliness and isolation.

Since (as was noted on p. 9 above) religious people have not generally been found to differ significantly from others in their dogmatism or other personality characteristics, it is hard to argue for any specifically religious effects on personality until it can be shown that a religion amplifies or isolates particular characteristics, such as fear of death. Although being religious predicts (low) pre-marital intercourse, (greater) authoritarianism and (greater) marital satisfaction, there are few simple linear relationships between religion and personality, probably because those who are either high or low in religiousness may be more similar to one another simply because of their commitment than either group is to those who are neutral or conventionally religious.

We might, therefore, reformulate the problem of religious personality in terms of the ways religious sentiments or feelings are managed (following Hood, 1978). This approach recognizes that religion is a part of life, so that it is not unusual for a psychiatric illness to be expressed through religious delusions or for religious ideas to be used to explain madness, whether as a punishment for wrong-doing, as a form of possession, or as a peculiar insight. Religious communities can also provide a haven for those who are disturbed or do not cope well with the world, and they can have a therapeutic value because of that. While religious institutions could carry those influences uniquely, religious (and other group) participation is itself linked to pyschological well-being and social integration, simply because it offers social involvement rather than isolation.

There are no directly *religious* reasons why those who attend church regularly should live longer than those who do not, unless church-going indicates a regular life-style, conservative attitudes, and is linked with good health through not drinking or living dangerously. Many tightly-knit groups, in particular Mormons and Seventh Day Adventists, do protect their members from life's excesses. For those who are active members of one of the main-line denominations, however, religion implies commitment, belonging, shared beliefs, social support and a network that can help them deal with adversity in such a way that it also maintains their health. In this sense, religion relieves the isolation that is so destructive for psychiatric and other patients, not because of their imaginary religious (and other) friends but because of the active support others give them. Any demonstration of direct relationships between religion, personality adjustment or mental health are therefore confounded by the numerous indirect social influences any religion carries with it.

Classical theories

The classical psychoanalytic view has, however, been that religious behaviour and psychoneurosis have much in common. As Freud wrote, 'mankind will overcome this neurotic phase, just as so many children grow out of their similar neurosis'. Although some religions appear bizarre to outsiders, so long as they are institutionally or socially sanctioned they are unlikely to be frankly pathogenic. Similarly, the firm diagnosis of a paranoid delusion about being an important person can only be made when there are no cultural sanctions for that belief. The classic studies of this have been in the alliances of small groups or minor prophetic movements. So, Festinger, Riecken and Schachter's book, *When Prophecy Fails* (1956), followed through the creation and slow dissolution of a quasi-religious group that formed around a Mrs Keech, who claimed to have received privileged information about the end of the world, and how one could be saved from that fate by following advice she had been given. Even when her predictions were proved wrong, it was several months before all her group members distanced themselves from her influence. In a similar way, since a valid psychiatric diagnosis can seldom be made simply from biological evidence, some consensus about whether a person is mad or not is needed to establish the validity of any such claims, and the distress experienced by those saying that they, or someone else, is disturbed or misled.

An unresolved question centres on the psychological or personality characteristics that might be needed to offer guarantees to someone else that a religious system is plausible, beyond having been trained into it from childhood. Conversion to Pentecostalism has become one domain in which those processes have been investigated, since speaking in tongues is ambiguous, but now quite widespread. When Malony and Lovekin (1985, Chapters 10 and 11) examined the evidence about the effects of Pentecostalism they concluded that because of biased judgements and the values of the investigators themselves, which cannot be easily controlled, and because personality characteristics depend on non-religious factors, no evidence can support conclusions that glossolalia consistently changes people either for the worse or for the better. Whatever effects there might be depend on the interaction between particular people and their religious contexts. Kildahl (1972) concluded that:

> As with many other experiences, the use to which glossolalia is put is often a reflection of emotional maturity. In our study persons with a low level of emotional stability tended to be extreme in their affirmation of the benefits of glossolalia. A well integrated 'tongue-speaker' generally made no wildly exaggerated claims for its powers, used it in a way that was not sensational, and did not allow it to dominate his life or use it as an instrument by which to manipulate others. (p. 59)

In short, the uses of these and other forms of religiousness depend on one's social needs and how they can be satisfied. Psychological interpretations also reflect the assumptions made by their investigators.

Religious maturity

While people who are psychologically 'mature' can be expected to be different from those who are immature, 'maturity' itself has been defined in many different ways, all of which involve conjectures and norms about what is 'best' (as Marie Jahoda, 1958, has shown). Since Christianity has its own models of maturity, independent information is needed about what it means to be mature in general and not just in religious terms (as was suggested on p. 25). Those judgements must also recognize the wide differences in the way people adjust and develop. More emphasis has been given to avoiding negative states like depression and anxiety, however, than to what might be constructive, because adversities are more easily recognized. But the boundaries between religious insight or attachment and insanity cannot be drawn rigidly, although among Pentecostals for example, it has been found that 'All the studies acknowledge that there is a real, even a radical, change in attitudes for those who become glossolalic' (Malony and Lovekin, 1985, p. 188). That these people describe positive changes in their attitudes (which caused Ronald Knox to write of Pentecostalism as a religious 'Enthusiasm') stresses an important difference between the findings from large-sample studies which must collapse their data across groups of people in order to identify general trends, and the accounts of outstanding individuals or cases who exemplify whatever might be recognized as a general process.

Countless studies of the characters of Luther, Wesley, Fox and other reformers have been based on one or another psychological theory, although whenever someone describes their own life, or that of another person, a few strands will be emphasized and a great deal omitted to make their story coherent. So Erik Erikson's *Young Man Luther* (1958) suggested that when Luther had a fit in the choir it was the turning point in his life, although other decisive events might equally well have been stressed. All autobiographies involve deliberate constructions of events to build a case either for or against a particular perspective, and this is especially so in relating religious histories. It is probably for this reason that being decentred, or detached (even from psychological theories), has been offered as a decisive criterion of maturity.

It is now obvious that religion was given a bad reputation by the early psychological studies that described religious believers as conforming, rigid, prejudiced, unintelligent and defensive. But in an analysis of the studies of religion and personality published up to 1979, Bergin (1983) found that twenty-three of them showed no relationship between religion and psychopathology, five showed a positive relationship and only two a negative relationship. While the theories which assume that psychopathology is a primary source of religious commitment are therefore almost certainly false, there is good evidence that religious involvement does help people to avoid social problems and that conversion to a 'new religion' is likely to improve one's social adjustment. (That conclusion is not universally agreed, although the arguments against it are more often made on principle than from sound evidence.) Although religion *is* multifaceted, it has been too easy to reduce religious devotion or belief and church attendance to the good or approved and the bad forms, or to oversimplify religiousness by dividing it into healthy and unhealthy types, without showing clearly what each one might involve. In the same way, it is an exaggeration to reduce the forms of psychopathology simply to psychosis and neurosis. Even the 'bad' kinds of religion might have positive effects on those who have found nothing else to rely on. The unanswerable question is therefore, What would religious people be like *without* their religious beliefs?

Summary

There is little support in studies of the links between personality and religion for any direct or simple relationship between them, despite the stereotype often found in our culture of religious people as suggestible, intolerant, narrow-minded and over-controlled. This is partly because of the 'hidden' variables, and especially the influence of religious groups and the roles they offer that prescribe what the members of such groups should be like.

Since comparatively few people have deliberately chosen their religious denomination, to argue for a close fit between religion and personality implies that personality (as a psychological structure that involves how we perceive, understand, think, and feel about ourselves and our environment) is always shaped by religion. This might apply to those who have chosen to adopt a particular religious position *because* it is congruent with their personal or social needs and not just on intellectual or social grounds. When a religion has been found plausible it can quite easily be integrated with the rest of life, and it might even become a dominant focus without influencing the aspects of personality that are usually measured. While autobiographical (and retrospective) accounts are still the only way that religious personalities can be fully described, those accounts are not independent of whatever social and religious processes they refer to. A similar difficulty confronts those who would relate (or align) mental disorder with religion, and any epidemiologically-based conclusions about the illnesses of Protestants, Catholics, Jews and others are hopelessly confounded because the incidence of severe mental disorder decreases with higher social status, which itself influences religious alignments and the social support that is available. Furthermore, 'being religious' can influence what one discloses, the ways experiences are interpreted, and therefore how personality and mental health are intertwined.

While the enthusiastic and controlling forms of religion can become either a haven or a challenge, very few studies have looked at 'religion' in that detail. Even were such studies to be available, few direct effects are likely to be uncovered, although it has been suggested, for example, that some of the medieval saints may have suffered from anorexia nervosa (Bell, 1985). Religious people who withdraw from the wider society, do not necessarily do so because they have had an emotional breakdown; many religious actions are more ambiguous than most arguments about them have allowed, except perhaps for the sick souls and divided selves that especially interested William James, and for those with a shallow commitment to religion. While deeply religious involvement implies some awareness of one's inadequacies, such self-knowledge is not restricted to religion.

A different view might hold that since religions are developed and applied to particular situations, personality characteristics must be irrelevant, apart from any effects of conformity to religious orthodoxies and the institutional pressures that maintain control over group members and support their beliefs. We therefore display our beliefs differently to those we expect to be hostile to them from the way we show them to fellow believers. Because of that alone it is almost impossible to find any direct relationships between personality and religion that are not trivial. Religious belief is, however, linked with social conservatism and with holding open- and closed- or tough- and tender-minded attitudes in tension. Any active religiousness is also expressed in social contexts and alignments that can easily accentuate differences between religious groups.

We do not need to fit the same psychological analysis to every believer, since each marks out his or her own solution within whatever constraints they accept. Confessors, counsellors or therapists may help those who cannot solve their own problems or unpack the 'invisible religion' that lies between the 79 per cent of the population who say they believe in God and the 22 per cent who go to church regularly, or that makes it easier for females than males to show that they are 'religious'.

6 Religion and Social Life

It is not the consciousness of man that determines our existence – rather, it is social existence that determines our consciousness.

after Karl Marx

The common emphasis on a separation of body and soul keeps religion locked within persons, at least until a worshipping community or the place of religion in society is mentioned. That religious institutions and ideas are so pervasive can be as much of a problem for psychology as it is for religion, because the balance between physical and mental factors seems to keep changing as much as it does between individuals and society. Even those 'born into' a religion may later reject it, despite the assumption that an individual's personality will interact strongly with their religious position. The evidence, however, supports the greater importance of external or social influences on one's choice of religion, especially since it is adults, and in particular parents, who provide religious models for children. Religious involvement can therefore be more easily predicted from a knowledge of people's social background and the religious tradition in which they were brought up than from information about their personalities.

Any Church and every church member exists within a social context. Despite that, the roots of religion have more often been looked for in the psychology of individuals than in their social or cultural background, or even in the historical development of their tradition, its control over credibility, and the specific effects of ethnic, denominational or doctrinal differences. The best psychological questions are not, however, historical (like 'Who made it?'). They are functional, asking 'Who can use it?' or 'What is religion for?' While the solutions to those problems must accept the interaction between individuals and society, we still need to know about their relative contribution to religiousness.

Social psychology

Psychology has recently changed, so that the role of social processes in constraining behaviour is increasingly being recognized. The sociology of religion, which concerns the way religion depends on, is changed by or adapts itself to a socio-cultural setting, has always been an important aspect of the scientific study of religion, one of the concerns of which is 'the unintended social repercussions of intentional human actions' (Popper, 1945, p. 95). Religions make an important contribution to the prescriptions and the proscriptions that control social interaction. They also define some of the consensual meanings that help to interpret experience and maintain cohesive social groups, despite the apparent decline of church-oriented religion in the western world.

Are we led to believe by a *system* that enforces its doctrines on us? Do we have the independence, or do we only imagine that we have the independence, to make up our own minds? (The concept of a 'false consciousness' suggests that we are socially controlled, but do not quite realize it.) The accepted rationality of religious doctrines is certainly sanctioned by tradition and sustained by the people who currently exercise control within that system. Revolutionary individuals and sectarian groups do, however, try to erode that established control, and sometimes succeed, despite the difficulties that stand in their way and the resilience of the traditions they challenge.

As well as being a cultural 'fact', religions involve the social organizations which Emile Durkheim, a founder of the sociology of religion, said unite those who share some 'body' of doctrines into a church which locks sacred and secular values together. The strong view, which holds that social systems dictate the beliefs and experience of individuals, therefore implies that it is not religion itself, but our consciousness and sense of independence that is illusory. A weaker view holds that it is individual members with particular positions, roles and beliefs who keep the organizational structures alive.

In religious terms this is partly a question of whether salvation is an individual or a social process, whether it depends on faith or on works that are themselves cast within some broader social context. In psychological terms the question is whether a craving for power or the benefits of life within a community are likely to be more social than individual. Even our most personal decisions are shaped and influenced by our social role or position. In producing a psychological explanation of religion it is therefore more parsimonious to assume that social life influences individuals (even if that influence is beyond their awareness) than to regard social and personal life as in any sense equivalent. Some social psychologists even argue that one function of our social attitudes is to specify social rules for conduct, so that attitudes then become explanations of action rather than statements about intentions or future actions.

Social involvement

Any active religious commitment necessarily involves an alignment with some institutions or groups and keeping our distance from others, but an individual's hostility to religion is not necessarily sanctioned by particular groups (such as 'youth for anti-Christ'). A person who, for example, rejects Catholicism may base his or her stance on a systematic opposition to Catholic doctrines or practice. One of the consequences of the realization that we usually need others' support for our views is to be found in Max Weber's distinction between churches and sects. Churches tend to be more open and apply less stringent criteria for membership than sects, which often aim to preserve 'purer' forms of what were originally church-based religions that are believed to have been compromised by their worldly success. Membership of a sect is therefore more socially restrictive than is membership of any church, since sects tend to reject their secular context.

This does not mean that all sects are similar in theological or even sociological terms. In fact there is continuing debate about how sects can be classified, and whether they put their emphasis on conversion, reform, revolution or withdrawal from the society within which they are cast. It has also been argued that sects give their members different satisfactions or rewards from those offered by churches, and make claims that can compensate for the social deprivations or deficiencies of their members. That argument is hard to test except among those who have been converted into such an exclusive group and expect to be rewarded. The reasons they might give for joining the sect are likely to be different from those that their observers will detect. For that reason alone, psychologists are usually cautious about untested explanations of why anyone engages in particular actions. Argyle and Beit-Hallahmi (1975) emphasized that there are too many kinds of deprivation to assume that either objectively established or felt deprivations in economic, social or personal domains have equivalent strength, or that any of them can be corrected simply by joining a religious group. Despite that, belonging to a 'special' group can itself be rewarding and improve one's perceived social status or increase one's sense of belonging to a community.

The parallel question of why people leave or give up their membership in a religious group or organization has been unduly neglected. Perhaps this is because most people drift away and do not explicitly 'leave' a religion unless they want to turn their resignation itself into a statement about themselves or against the organization's policies and practice. The religion of the majority of people is community or ethnically based rather than a strongly personal commitment or identity.

Caplovitz and Sherrow (1977) found in a Canadian study that about 12 per cent of Jews and Protestants and about 6 per cent of Catholics deliberately drop out from their religion and do not join another. One of my recent Australian studies found that 48 per cent of a sample of university students said they had simply 'given up' their family's religion. Their own explanations for this involved a mixture of political reasons, personal dissatisfaction, intellectual doubt and domestic or social circumstances, which were accentuated when the time came for them to leave home. It seems unreasonable to expect that everyone will find religious groups congenial. Those who switch from one denomination to another may do so for religious or for social reasons, with the usual direction of change being towards a tradition with higher status and less stringent demands unless other social factors such as friendship or marriage are involved. In general, a higher education and economic status go with a more formal accept-ance of religious belief. Despite that, the theologically more conserva-tive churches, with their greater expected commitment, continue to grow.

Membership in religious organizations can provide personal and social satisfaction not only because of their recognized solutions to universal problems, but also for the direct benefits of their social and institutional support. Public or communal alignments with religion are therefore consistent with widely divergent underlying beliefs, even about the benefits of those alignments.

Social surveys

Survey data have been used to test whether the social functions of religion are to comfort people or to challenge them (using Glock et al.'s (1967) contrast), to show that the conservative churches are growing, and to measure the effects of an education in a denominational or state school on the religion of adults. Surveys have also been used by churches (and others) to help to change attitudes by showing what a majority believes, and to research their own 'market' by identifying existing agreements. The answers found in these studies show the support that is directly available within established social or religious structures but neglect functional analyses of the personal goals that religion can help to fulfil.

While religious doctrines are public and formally specified, religious *beliefs* are, like religious experiences, diffuse and held by individuals. Although beliefs usually reflect accepted doctrines, the ways they deviate from orthodox positions can be hard to detect because the answers to a questionnaire or other inquiry will often be adjusted to support or attack the interests of whatever group has sanctioned the investigation. Respondents are aware of what they are expected to say or agree to as they distinguish the meaning of their beliefs or actions from their social consequences. The implications of these social sanctions for a person's experience and practice are often unclear because of that, even when a religion maintains moral values and holds groups or societies together through the roles they give to those who preserve and carry ideals about the transcendent.

The old argument that contemporary forms of religion have evolved from primitive or archaic forms obscured the extent to which traditional practices *must* be recreated by individuals if they are to remain plausible. But that seems easier to do in rural than urban settings, and within a family, especially when the mother is religiously active. To 'let go' of religion is easiest for those who have moved away from home or when it has not been emphasized there.

Max Weber's historical and sociological perspective on religious change linked the growth of the work ethic in capitalist societies with the growth of Protestantism in the late seventeenth century. There is, however, little psychological evidence to suggest that a specific alliance between Protestantism and capitalism continues to operate, not least because the attitudes to work and success among Catholics and Jews are now similar to those of Protestants (Furnham, 1984). Despite that finding, this controversy has been an important one because it raises questions about the relationships between religious doctrines and ideas and social innovation or restraint.

Attitudes to contraception offer an important instance of this. Because Roman Catholic authorities have steadfastly continued to hold that abortion and the use of artificial methods of birth control are wrong, despite the changing attitudes to these questions (with which the Protestant churches have largely acquiesced), they have increased the tension among their members. American studies of contraceptive use in 1955 and 1976 showed that while 52 per cent of Protestants aged 18–29 used *some* method of contraception in 1955 and 61 per cent of the same age-group used some method in 1976, 39 per cent of Catholics used some contraceptive in 1955 compared with 64 per cent in 1976, the pill being the preferred method for both religious groups in the later survey (cf. Mosher and Goldscheider, 1984). In 1965, 24 per cent of the British population was totally opposed to abortion, but in 1971 that figure had dropped to 7 per cent. Findings like these emphasize changed attitudes, and also an inconsistency between the strict attitudes to moral questions of church authorities and common practice. About three-quarters of the British population say they would be prepared to agree to abortion in certain circumstances, such as if the baby would be born deformed or the pregnancy had resulted from rape or incest. Nevertheless, a study of Catholic attitudes to abortion in Sydney in 1978 showed that while the patterns of pregnancy and abortion do not differ between Catholics and Protestants (despite the formal differences in their ideologies), when those data were broken down to distinguish practising from non-practising Catholics, it was found that 90 per cent of the Catholics who had had an abortion were non-practising.

Community attitudes over the last fifteen years have moved away from rigid rules for conduct towards greater respect for individual responsibility, especially in the attitudes reflected in reduced legal sanctions towards nudity, masturbation and homosexuality. Gorsuch and Smith (1972) showed that from 1939 to 1969, it was only judgements about sexual behaviour in their fifty-item list that became less severe over this period. Nevertheless, Morrison (1985) in a comprehensive review of 'adolescent contraceptive behaviour' noted the continued importance of religious objections to contraceptive use, and that while differences between the denominations are quite small, within Protestant groups these differences depend on a liberal-conservative distinction and the frequency of church attendance, which again appears to reinforce a religious conservatism.

That these social attitudes are still vulnerable to entrenched and conservative pressure groups is emphasized by the 1986 United States government report on pornography which reversed the liberal conclusions of the 1970 American Surgeon-General's Commission, finding that pornography should be controlled because of its adverse effects. Disagreements with that conclusion stress the social tension surrounding the specific actions that are allowable in this, as in other, domains. Recent public controversies about 'safe sex', especially in relation to AIDS and its causes, have emphasized other differences in attitudes within the churches.

Group processes in religion

During and after the 1950s psychologists became interested in the ways social groups and the mere presence of other people dominate the decisions individuals make, especially in situations that seem ambiguous. These pressures, which work to produce a group coherence that defines what is 'correct', depend importantly on the group's size and composition. For example, Wicker and Mehler (1971) found that newcomers to a Methodist church in the United States with 338 members found themselves more rapidly assimilated to it than did newcomers to a comparable church with 1,599 members, when assimilation was assessed by their participation in its activities, feeling obliged to participate, developing a sense of belonging, and becoming acquainted with other church members and officers. Such studies emphasize the importance of the setting in which behaviour takes place, and could explain why small churches in rural areas are more efficient in maintaining contact with their parishioners than are large city churches. Other studies have shown that religious similarity is an important criterion of our attraction to other people and that, given the opportunities, friendships develop within religious (and similar) groups.

Findings like these depend on the fact that social groups are constituted by those who share a common social identity, and regard themselves as belonging to the same social category. Language, religion and ethnicity (which is often aligned with a religion) are robust personal identifiers that explicitly support the social cohesion that flows from sharing experiences, perspectives, and such things as dress or diet, and from explicit signs of having been initiated into membership – by circumcision, for example. A study in Northern Ireland by Stringer and Cairns (1983) of reactions amongst school children to a set of stereotyped Catholic and Protestant faces showed that Protestants aged 14–15 rated the Protestant faces more favourably than they rated the Catholic faces, although Catholics rated both sets of faces similarly. Those positive in-group evaluations among the Protestants were, however, made by members of the majority group there.

Concepts of the self and of other people which depend on a membership in formal social groups involve categories like sex, nationality, occupation and religiousness to identify the 'socio-demographic' and class-based features of their members. Psychological attributes or traits, such as competence, introversion or extraversion, and interests or values, while being personal are also shared with others in the same or different groups, or they are assigned to those who carry out appropriate tasks. Since a religious identity is an important component of the self concept, many who are religiously inactive retain a religious identity that they switch on in appropriate situations, while the clergy and other church officials are expected to maintain that identity consistently.

Social relations within a group depend on mutual attraction and cohesion, emotional support, co-operation, as well as some attitudinal and behavioural uniformity, as individuals fulfil stereotypic social roles. This itself accounts for the frequently observed conservatism of religious and other institutions, and anyone marginal to 'their' religion acts cautiously because they are unsure of the religious norms they *should* observe. Those who are 'unchurched' are in their turn typed in ways that include being 'rebels', 'burnt-out', 'locked-out', or 'true unbelievers'.

Summary

While non-psychologists are likely to define the religious commitment of individuals in personal terms, religious attachments never take place in a social vacuum. Part of their context is defined by the religious traditions maintained by organizations having the features of a church, sect, or cult. A solitary religious figure is almost a contradiction in terms. While religious systems recognize that God deals with individuals as members of societies, or with 'chosen' groups, sociologists explore how those groups relate to the rest of society and study how any society deals with religious organizations; they tend to neglect how organizations deal with their individual members. Weber's distinction between church and sect therefore focused on the requirements for membership, with sects being more restrictive, stringent and isolated from their society than churches, which are more open, tolerant and compromised to the world.

This lack of openness means that there has been less study of sects and their members than of churches, although it is possible for break-away sects to revitalize or reform a church, as they polarize 'in-group/out-group' distinctions. While sociologists have described the close connections between church-based and religious or social variables like age, sex and occupation, they have relied either on social deprivation theory, secularization or the competition for control and social change to explain how religious individuals or groups survive. Dittes (1971) noted that 'Among social scientists, one would be hard pressed to find any major theorist who did *not* formulate his understanding of religion as a compensation for deprivation'. Those deprivations may be social (as Marx believed) or personal (as in Freud's theory). The *evidence* for a deprivation theory of religion is, however, weak.

Psychologists, on the other hand, have looked at the social functions of religion, at the consequences of involvement with it and the identity it gives.

That secular influences might be 'winning' over religion is shown by the declining support that religious groups are thought to receive. But what support *are* they still given? While it is beyond our scope to examine this, church-based religions are adjusting their demands and their forms (if slowly) by reducing their demands for exclusivity and sexual purity, so leaving sects and a sect-like conservatism to look after the exclusive forms of religion.

Religion is inevitably a culturally-bound phenomenon (as the liberation theologies emphasize). While the actual statistics vary from place to place, country to country and across denominations, social processes inevitably influence what can be practised by individuals. That Catholicism shows consistently higher participation rates than Protestantism, or that America's religions are more diverse than those in Europe, is easily explained historically and by reference to the role of ethnic churches in assimilation or to their other direct social roles – in conducting funerals, for example. Pluralism and the privatization of religion might take people away from the Church, but not from religion.

It is hard to escape the conclusion that while modern religions can be understood as archaic, romantic vestiges, with little place in a modern society, they are protected, respected and continue to be called on when people are in crisis. The networks and social relationships they foster and their specific sanctions give them an important role that helps to fix social identities. The moral and social 'careers' offered by religion help individuals to explain and confront problems with a logic that focuses on personal behaviour, belief and experience, and stresses the priority of institutions that tell us whether God is within us or outside, as we struggle with ourselves or with the world, either on a ladder or moving in a circle. Whatever solutions are found appealing must be socially sanctioned, since they help to maintain the social order and our relationships with other people.

7 Beliefs and Attitudes

I believe in God . . .

The Apostles' Creed

I believe because it is impossible.

Tertullian

Belief is the central problem in the analysis of mind.

Bertrand Russell

While social contexts, traditions and institutions define what religion can be, they also structure or prescribe what individuals can legitimately do with it. A plausible orthodoxy or consensus is needed to support the usually positive (but also negative) orientations to the variety of religious doctrines and practices that are available, and to identify what the practitioners will decide is credible. Unlike factual beliefs that can be tested in the 'real' world, religious beliefs are supported by social agreements and traditions. Once accepted, those beliefs are displayed in ways that allow others to decide who is truly religious, hypocritical, sceptical, agnostic, mistaken and so on. It is hard to validate those judgements independently of an interaction between persons and their beliefs, although 'belief' is a prototypic psychological category and we usually allow people to make claims about their own beliefs. Psychologists define beliefs operationally in terms of the confidence that is expressed in them, leaving to philosophers the difficult problems of deciding where boundaries between belief and knowledge might lie, and whether believing is different from seeing, denying, doubting or 'opining'.

We can only confidently establish what people believe by asking them. Since they do not have to be truthful in what they say, we also rely on what they *do*, – such as going to church or backing a horse – to confirm our hunches about their credibility. Despite that, important distinctions between belief 'in' a person and the belief 'that' an event has occurred could entail different states of mind or levels of confidence. We have already seen that religious beliefs such as whether Christianity is a 'better' religion than Buddhism are accepted or rejected more confidently than are factually verifiable statements such as whether there are tigers in China (p. 11). Moral beliefs and values draw yet other support because of the regulative and meta-beliefs we hold about their rationality. These world-views and beliefs must be shared with others, or we might be identified as mad; and what we believe must make enough intellectual and emotional sense to compel our own conviction.

While most European adults believe they are free to choose their beliefs and children expect to be told what to believe, some cultures and groups hold it legitimate to enforce certain beliefs on some of their adult members, at least in public. Religious groups with their sure grasp of 'truth' similarly may give themselves the power to coerce the beliefs of their members, sometimes making the distinction between education and indoctrination hard to draw. While 'we' educate, 'they' often indoctrinate. Disbelief and incredulity about the elements of a doctrinal system increases with a lack of coherence among specific beliefs, or when their social sanctions are withdrawn. But social processes are usually so potent that even then disconfirmation of religious beliefs is often resisted.

Distinctions are commonly made between beliefs about oneself, about the facts of nature and the social world, and about the norms for conduct. Behind them all are the authorities that support them, whether through personal experience and reason, or by fiat, tradition or consensus. Beliefs about our sex, name, and physical powers have therefore been described as 'primitive' because we do not remember when we acquired them, and they are self-referential. Most other beliefs that involve predictions about the stability or consistency of the world are 'derived', even if we are so strongly convinced about them that they have become part of our conception of 'self'. Other uses of the word 'belief' extend beyond those distinctions to include statements like 'I believe what you say (but disagree with you)' and 'I believe (expect or hope) she will call me'.

The phenomenology of religious beliefs is characterized by their diversity, strength or polarization, potency, and sanctioning authorities. They are also readily identified from their content or stylistic features as being radical or conservative, tough or tender-minded, institutional or individualistic, and tolerant or intolerant. While even unusual beliefs are expected to be testable, they are often directly evaluated against prejudices about the state of mind or plausibility of their advocates, who may be recognized as 'cranks' simply because of what they seem to believe.

Unlike the forms of knowledge that can be demonstrated in skills or knowing how to do things, beliefs are conveyed verbally. While most common nouns have agreed meanings, religious terms like God, sin or soul draw varying support and their core social meanings can be idiosyncratically (and connotatively) elaborated. Such additional meanings have been studied using a semantic differential procedure, in which the target words are rated on sets of descriptive adjectives (like active-passive, fast-slow and good-bad). As we have seen (p. 6) this procedure has shown that the concept of God is as closely aligned with positive female as with male characteristics. Despite such deeper meanings, in the United States 94 per cent of those older than 18 say they believe in God (without having been asked to identify the kind of god they believe in), and 57 per cent hold that their religious beliefs are 'very important' to them (Princeton Religious Research Center, 1979–80). In a recent study at the University of New South Wales, 59 per cent of a sample of 786 students said they belong to an identified religion, 12 per cent said they had a 'personal religion', 22 per cent said they had 'no religion' and 7 per cent said they were atheists. Because of the extraordinary stability about these patterns of affiliation and acceptance within a society and their small changes across time, the relevance of these self-identifications cannot be expected to change.

We must therefore distinguish assent to a proposition (such as 'I believe in God the Father') from the meaning it carries beyond any formal doctrinal content. For that reason, we may find that we disagree with someone who appears to hold beliefs similar to our own because of the emphasis they have given to them. But people who read the same book find different meanings there if one reads it as history and another as a novel. In a similar sense, materialists and transcendentalists, or fundamentalists and those with a metaphorical understanding of religious truth, can find it harder to agree on the implications of concepts like the resurrection than on belief in God, because of the guarantees they use to structure the doctrines, as well as the support they claim for the beliefs they accept.

Surface structures

Measures of religion have tended to confuse beliefs and attitudes when asking for the degree of agreement with statements like 'Christ died for sinners', 'The Ten Commandments were good for people of olden times but are really not applicable to modern life' and the other statements that we mentioned in Chapter Three. Beliefs are identified with subjective certainty about the truth of a proposition or doctrine on what are implicitly considered adequate grounds, while attitudes are 'learned predispositions to respond in a consistently favourable or unfavourable manner towards particular social objects'. It is fairly obvious that our attitudes to religious beliefs must be measured with a focus on their generally accepted meanings, and that their implications or consequences for particular individuals demand careful study.

While religious believers adopt a doctrinal position, unbelievers may identify religion itself, as well as the doctrines and their believers, as 'irrational' or 'stupid'. That may be an existentially important distinction which matters little if the aim of a study is to find how religious beliefs and attitudes are themselves structured. King and Hunt (1975), who made a careful analysis of the religious domain, identified the following separate components there:

a) credal assent (as in the statement, 'I believe that the word of God is revealed in the Scriptures'),
b) devotionalism (in the practice of prayer),
c) church attendance,
d) organizational activity,
e) financial support,
f) religious despair (as in, 'My personal existence often seems meaningless and without purpose'),
g) the salience of religion,
h) cognitive style, as in closeness to God or an intolerance of ambiguity,
i) a purpose in life.

In several replications among separate 'main-line Protestant' groups they found that while these factors are conceptually independent of each other, they are positively related. This suggests that a positive, general attitude to religion underlies these separate measures, although credal assent, intolerance of ambiguity, and the purpose of life did form a separate cluster with little relation to the measures of religious participation. We can therefore accept the conclusion that religious belief and practice tend to be separate aspects of religion.

Thouless (1935) used a different approach when he distinguished in principle the beliefs about God (as in, 'There is a personal God' and, 'The world was created by God') and Christ ('Jesus Christ was God the Son' and, 'Jesus changed water into wine') from other orthodox Christian beliefs ('There is a personal Devil' and, 'The spirits of human beings continue to exist after the death of their bodies') and from general religious beliefs ('Matter is not the sole reality' and, 'There are such spiritual beings as angels'). As well as those beliefs, Thouless assessed religious attitudes or opinions ('Religion is the opium of the people' and, 'Man is, in some degree, responsible for his actions'), factual assertions ('The universe is expanding', 'Moses was the author of the first five books of the Bible', and, 'Green is a primary colour') and a few miscellaneous beliefs including 'Belief in evolution is compatible with belief in a Creator'. Thouless found much greater confidence, whether for or against the religious items, than about the statements of fact. It has been found, in subsequent work, that while 92 per cent of a sample of Roman Catholics expressed complete certainty about their belief in God, only 23 per cent of those who said they had no religion were completely certain of their disbelief. Data from groups of religious and non-religious students in Australia, in which their religious and non-religious beliefs and attitudes as well as neuroticism or anxiety were assessed, showed a religious belief factor (which accounts for 43 per cent of the variance) and a neuroticism or anxiety factor that is independent of religious belief but is related to confidence in the factual items. That study gives further support to the independence and the coherence of religious belief.

There are many other studies like these, which Spilka, Hood and Gorsuch (1985) summarize by saying that, 'In our culture, it appears that religious and non-religious (people who could be) Christians are distinguished (from each other) by being intrinsically committed to a basically traditional, Gospel-oriented interpretation of Christianity, which is, however, not identical to fundamentalism' (p. 50). Those who can be identified as religious people have also been found to differ in terms of their intrinsic-extrinsic, law-based rather than prophecy-based and individualistic or institutional orientations.

Although social psychologists have assumed that attitudes imply a predisposition to react positively to objects that are related to particular issues, Fishbein and Ajzen (1974) showed that when attitudes towards religion were correlated with the intention to perform each of several separate religious behaviours, like donating money to a religious institution or praying before or after meals, the average correlation between religious attitudes and the intention to act on them was only .17. That is low because any intention to perform an action is limited by contextual factors, opportunities, and how separate different religious actions are. Someone might go to church regularly and pray before meals, but not want to give money to a particular church or to sing in its choir. The only general tendency to translate religious beliefs or intentions into action refers to church attendance itself.

Ostrom (1969) therefore found that church attendance was the only religious behaviour he could predict with reasonable accuracy from separate measures of the cognitive, affective and intentional components of religion. Furthermore, Jean-Pierre Deconchy (1980) found that when a group of Catholics answered a belief questionnaire they thought came from a Protestant group they showed a high degree of agreement among themselves, although their answers to a similar questionnaire from a Catholic source showed greater variability, probably because they took it as an opportunity to show their disagreement with official doctrines. Consistent with that is Wicker's (1971) finding that the influence of specific extraneous events (like having weekend guests who did not regularly attend church, or finding that their church contributions were being used for a project they disapproved of) were good predictors of non-participation in church activities. This again emphasizes the influence of contextual factors on the way religion is expressed, since the setting and the occasion, purpose, obligations and actions required do not often correspond. Simple changes in intention can prevent any action from being carried out.

Findings like these suggest that while a person's degree of religiousness can be evaluated, what that involves beyond being either for or against religion is neither self-evident nor easily displayed, except in circumstances that include no hint of criticism, or among those who are very strongly committed to evangelism. The pressures towards religious conformity are powerful because of our over-learned familiarity with stereotyped religious appeals and rituals.

Free-response answers are necessary if we are to study single individuals. When students have been asked to describe their beliefs or to write about what religion means for them they usually refer directly to a belief-disbelief dimension. Some convey an extrinsic or explicitly self-serving and conventional religion, while others describe intrinsic and strongly committed attitudes to the ways they make sense of religious doctrines, deferring to an external authority or to personal experience and the conviction that supports their religion.

These descriptions are inevitably influenced by personal judgements and social norms about what can be said about different contexts, and by what is still poorly described as an 'interest' in whatever forms the crux of their religious perspectives on life. A non-doctrinal religious perspective was identified by Yinger (1977) with reference to fundamental problems of meaninglessness, suffering and injustice, in the answers to questions about the most 'basic and permanent question for mankind'. There is some circularity there, since a group of Australian students who acknowledged those issues also tended to accept conventional Christian doctrines.

It may be that in the search to define the strength of someone's religiousness we have overlooked how religion is expressed, and how conflicts about it are resolved. That would involve identifying the contexts and the issues that are expected to require religious solutions, and the resources needed to solve them. Most measures of religion seem to have simply used Christian doctrines as slogans that can be recognized, and as guides to the practice of a majority, or as statements of the principles that could direct one's life, especially when confronted by particular social or personal problems.

Religious knowledge

It is agreed that Christian education is an important activity for churches and church schools, and that some minimum religious knowledge is needed to support a religious commitment. The doctrines or tenets, and the rituals of a religion, must be recognized before they can be believed and practised unless religious belief is to be blind.

Questions about religious and other kinds of knowledge are, however, difficult for most people to answer because of their lack of sophistication or training. Direct questions about politics and similarly 'complex' issues make people defensive whenever they are asked about their knowledge or belief, especially if they are unable to answer correctly. Such questions are readily seen to be challenging, since many people leave their 'general knowledge' behind as soon as they escape from formal schooling and can become opinionated.

For whatever reasons, there has been little systematic study of religious knowledge, except for its links with religious teaching. Those who would argue that religion either satisfies a 'need to know' or involves a continuing quest for ultimate answers might be advised to look initially at those whose only search is for dogmatic solutions. Since more than two-thirds of American Christians in a 1984 Gallup poll did not know who delivered the Sermon on the Mount, it seems pointless to ask samples of that population for their accounts or interpretations of what it was about. But what religious knowledge are we expected to have? Stark and Glock (1968, p. 161) concluded that: 'The public on the whole is amazingly ignorant of what seem to be unbelievably obvious questions. For example, 79 per cent of the Protestants and 86 per cent of the Catholics could not name a single Old Testament prophet, and more than a third did not know where Jesus was born.' They also noted that 'virtually everyone has a denomination, but few know even trivial facts about their faith' (p. 162).

When Stark and Glock asked people to identify whether each of a set of statements was from the Bible or not, they found that the language itself was confusing: 28 per cent of Protestants and 41 per cent of Catholics thought that 'Blessed are the strong: for they shall be the sword of God' was from the Bible, although almost all agreed that 'Blessed are the meek: for they shall inherit the earth' was biblical.

Perhaps the churches themselves have not encouraged firm religious knowledge, preferring to support positive evaluations of doctrines that are not to be questioned but accepted categorically. As well as looking at the people who decide to accept a religion, the reasons for their doctrinal assent deserves more critical study than it has been given – one might ask people what evidence would make them reject belief in, for example, life after death.

While the classical arguments for God's existence no longer bring many people to belief, we do not know what 'evidence' they would accept: and we have seen that Wittgenstein pointed out that expressing belief in a last judgement is not the same as asking if there is an aeroplane overhead.

Belief (or hope) may therefore be central to a personal religion. The assertions that 'illness is a punishment for sin', or, 'Jesus is the Son of God who rose from the dead' draw various degrees of agreement (or hoped-for belief). Yet specific disagreements are seldom strong enough to destroy a whole doctrinal system, and perhaps it is the language in which religious propositions are couched that evokes more support than their actual content. Nevertheless, belief without evidence is usually rejected as prejudice. While different explanations and accounts can change the meaning of an event in the real world, a great variety of mythical (and scientific) stories about the creation of the world can be woven together (or held apart), depending on our imagination and knowledge. In the same way, there are many other explanations than wilfulness and original sin for not believing in God or for acting inappropriately. The fact that the applications of religion, rather than its knowledge base, are emphasized both in church teaching and in psychological studies seems to parallel the ways a popular interest in religion has been constructed.

An inevitable conclusion from this work is that religious beliefs are assumed by many people to be 'primitive' or axiomatic, in the sense of being unquestioned (but not necessarily unanalysable) and rather like postulates in mathematics or science. While such beliefs can be examined or justified, and must be internally coherent, the majority of people do not question their validity. Support for religion is therefore likely to be found in experience or with reference to an authority, whether that is the Bible, church teaching, or the influence of an exemplary person. Some religious beliefs may be like phobias and 'irrational' fears because no external evidence (whether given by a friend or someone in authority) can disconfirm them. In that sense, as Rokeach (1960, p. 41) emphasized, each of the innumerable beliefs we hold has other beliefs associated with it that involve consensus estimates about how many people might accept these beliefs, and how attractive such support is.

Religious beliefs are therefore aligned less with our knowledge than with more primitive beliefs, including the beliefs in a just world (following Lerner, 1980) or in altruism (cf. Batson and Ventis, 1982) which have recently been used to investigate some consequences of a religious perspective experimentally (cf. p. 40 above). Rokeach (1960) has also argued that beliefs entail related disbeliefs, as well as central-peripheral and time-based or universal perspectives. While a believer's credibility can be doubted on the basis of what is or is not to be done as a consequence of whatever is claimed, religious beliefs are hard to question, except on traditional, logical or prejudiced grounds.

In an unusual study, Harrel (1977) interviewed sixty-six Taiwanese villagers about their traditional religious beliefs, and identified only a small group of 'true believers'. A few others were judged to be totally committed because no data could challenge their convictions, while some 'nonbelievers' had replaced traditional religious doctrines with either a scientific ideology or with naturalistic explanations. The largest groups he found there included 'practical believers' who relied on the usefulness of their beliefs, and the 'intellectual believers' for whom religion made their world intellectually coherent and orderly.

Conversion and change

The effects of religious revivals which rely on a challenging evangelism led William James to distinguish once-born Christians, who had grown into their faith, from the twice-born who, with a different temperament (as he thought), were compelled to accept or realize their faith within an instant.

The early psychologists of religion were fascinated by the phenomena of sudden conversion, and used it as their key to understanding the forms of religion they found in personal documents, interviews and questionnaires. In answering a questionnaire that had been widely distributed by J. B. Pratt in 1904, William James, when asked whether religion personally meant 'an emotional experience' replied, 'Not powerfully so, yet a social reality'. In answer to the question, 'What do you mean by a "religious experience"?', James wrote, 'Any moment of life that brings the reality of spiritual things more "home" to one'. This strong sense of reality and immediacy, which is usually analysed unwillingly by those who have it, pervades Pentecostalism and the 'new religious movements', as well as the conservative or 'sterner' forms of Christianity that stress sin and guilt. Such immediacy has been easily understood in doctrinaire psychological terms with reference to the resolution of a crisis and the sense of depersonalization or lack of identity that was thought to be common in adolescence, or the emotional conflict that results from an appeal based on fear, or in group-based and social expectations.

All of those factors could be reduced to a contrast between voluntary and forced or elicited decisions. While these explanations overlap and have become part of our definition of conversion, they involve notions about the reorientation, self-realization or conviction that can develop under social pressure or persuasion. Personality-based explanations of conversion and other sudden changes are especially familiar to psychiatrists, and refer back to William Sargant's analysis of a *Battle for the Mind* (1957/1971), which rests on neuro-physiological arguments about maintaining a balance between the excitatory and inhibitory processes which control appropriate levels of response to environmental stimuli. Excessively strong stimulation produces paradoxical responses, as when a small change in them generates profound emotional feelings which cause a switch, so that we 'become attached to ideas, faiths and persons previously despised' (p. 11), or produce the well-described feelings of being 'possessed' by ideas and even by other people.

An American psychiatrist, Jerome D. Frank (1961), in a study of *Persuasion and Healing*, also examined the psychological and social similarities between religious conversion, 'brainwashing' and psychotherapeutic processes. He argued that psychological and social factors alone cannot account for such changes, so that some predisposition or willingness to be changed must be postulated, usually with a sense of tension or dissatisfaction that can later be understood or solved religiously. For that to happen, agents of change must not only be encountered at a point of crisis, but their influences must be supported with strong social attachments to other committed believers, reduced contact with nonbelievers, and an expectation about the power of the new system.

Conversion to one of the 'new religious movements' is too easily understood in these terms. While some believe that the life of people who have been converted is often better than it was previously, outcries against the Moonies, Hare Krishna or other groups for their mercenary demands and apparent control over their converts has led a few to make dramatic efforts to 'spring' friends or relatives from those cults and 'reprogramme' them (Singer, 1979).

Obvious controversies surround those who suddenly change their ideology or group membership, whether they move in or out of a religion, occupation, marriage, or a friendship. Such changes are often interpreted or explained by observers or onlookers as having been unexpected and surprising, whatever the plans, goals, intentions or reasons that those who are involved might offer. But mere observation of them can never reveal their 'whole story', which must be filled in with the justifications, accounts and explanations that are necessary to preserve an intact social order. Each person's view of their own life history or 'career' will be at the centre of those accounts.

Deviant or unexpected actions can be restructured when they are explained by claims that they were accidental and unintended, solved another problem, were by-products of altruism and so on. Our theories about people and their reasons for action, as well as the plausibility of those reasons all determine whether an explanation is accepted. Explanations are often given in terms of 'motives' that appeal to an apparently fixed ground, like a biological drive or habit. While some religious groups seek to control biological functions by fasting or other forms of mortification, there is no evidence that that could itself *cause* someone to turn to religion, although it might put them into a state of ecstasy that can be interpreted in religious terms. While we often act without an awareness of what we are doing, to have been converted by an evangelist itself justifies or explains a change in one's life. To maintain that change can, however, be a problem, even with good models to follow, if strong social involvement and support is lacking. The early work which found that adolescents were the ones most likely to be converted, and then assumed that that was due to some biological factor associated with puberty, disregarded the extent to which young people were *expected* to 'see the light' and become responsible for themselves as they were growing into young adults. Many psychological explanations often disregard more obvious reasons.

It is usual for religious development to be a slow and not a rapid process, with its critical phases recognized only in retrospect. Godin (1964) has described an extreme instance. A Belgian priest who left a manuscript, that was published in 1904 twenty-five years after his death, described the gradual but apparently total loss of his faith. He explained that he had not changed the exterior signs of his belonging to the Church, even to other clergy, because of the help and comfort he felt he was able to give as a priest, which became the purpose of his existence. In a similar way, many specific 'reasons' can be given for going to Mass or lighting a votive candle, and leave those actions highly ambiguous. We must always ask the person involved what they thought they were doing before questioning the validity of their actions. Subjective information *is* always very important.

Nevertheless, comparisons of the social characteristics of those who have and have not given up the religion they grew up in can also expose consistencies that are easily missed in single case studies and self-descriptions. The detail of those consistencies must, however, be interpreted against implicit knowledge of what is socially possible (and acceptable). In an Australian study 36 per cent of a large student group said they had switched from a religious affiliation to no affiliation, although separate religious groups differed sharply in tl.e proportions who had left them, with 45 per cent among the Anglicans, 43 per cent of other Protestants, 33 per cent of Roman Catholics and 13 per cent among Jews having claimed a change. The 14 per cent who had moved from one denomination to another tended to follow agreed similarities between their present and future denominations and they gave reasons for changing in ideological, social, or aesthetic terms.

Rokeach (1960, p. 296) studied the similarity ratings that were made by the members of six Christian groups who were unanimous in ranking Jews, Muslims and then atheists as least similar to themselves. Among specific Christian groups the rank order given by Baptists was the reverse of that among Catholics, whose order was from Episcopalians to Lutherans, Presbyterians, Methodists, and then Baptists. Stark and Glock (1968) also found that the stability of church membership in California varies from one denomination to another. Episcopalians were the most stable group, with 83 per cent who had not changed, while the least stable were Congregationalists, 65 per cent of whom had become members of another denomination. Denominations also differ in their ability to attract members from other groups, although there is a general trend for people to move from more theologically conservative to more liberal groups, which Stark and Glock argue is related to their higher social status.

The profound differences between an active church membership and merely claiming to belong to a denomination is a neglected aspect of both the psychology and the sociology of religion. They can show the effects of social contexts and intentions on the religious careers that are available, which inevitably balance social pressures and aspirations against the accepted plausibility of religious doctrines and practices. While trends in the census data on religious affiliation in Australia and New Zealand show a consistent decrease in those claiming some denominational membership over the last ten years, it is not sensible to extrapolate that trend forward to predict that the churches will soon lose all their members. A few optimists see the changes promising a new 'inculturation' of religion in society if the churches can recapture their relevance to contemporary life. But most debates about the future of the Church take place in the absence of social science evidence about how the Church is reacted to socially and personally; from a psychological perspective this entails understanding the meaning that can be found in religious doctrines and the uses that can be made of them, beyond whatever support they give to moral principles and social involvement.

Just as the traditional beliefs about religious and other experiences have changed, psychological explanations are not independent of implicit judgements about the nature of our psychological science and whether its theories should be concerned with reactions to what is 'outside' and in the social environment, or internal and involved with emotions or feelings and the nature of understanding.

It has become fashionable to emphasize that shared systems of belief are necessary to maintain cohesive social groups and counteract an 'ontological anxiety' by giving prepared answers to many 'Why?' questions. The blinding insights that some people have reported could be illusory, and even religious belief systems include ways to account for our failures that help to control the environment in terms of God's punishment, social injustice, or through our own grievous faults. 'Why me?' still seems an inevitable question whenever misfortune strikes. The answers that religious people give 'can encompass an incident of seeming injustice within the larger framework of ultimate justice, (so that) in effect, there are no innocent victims, no injustices, in the ultimate scheme of things' (Lerner, 1980, p. 164).

Christians can find many models among the prophets and martyrs to support that belief. When other hopes fail there appears little alternative to an appeal to the supernatural or to fate, chance, and other more ultimate concepts. Lerner argues that these are universal processes. He justifies this with evidence about the competition among self-centred individuals for scarce resources, as they preserve their belief in a just world, and through the subjective and objective implications of that for their own position. Although Lerner's is not a cynical analysis, it emphasizes the self-interest that supports any 'effort after the meaning' of what we have experienced. Theological interpretations of the Fall, as a myth about the natural state of mankind, emphasize beliefs that structure the natural world in terms of the supernatural, while other moral stories conclude that 'As ye sow, so shall ye reap', as a way to preserve good behaviour.

An example of prejudiced beliefs is found in the apparently inevitable assumption that 'true believers' are authoritarian and conventional. A more contemporary view holds that processing transcendental experience and knowledge is, like music or painting, mediated primarily by the right hemisphere of the brain (in right-handed people), with analytic and verbal control located in the left hemisphere. This theory argues that fundamentally non-verbal, non-conceptual but direct experiences are translated into the language of religious doctrine and dogma, which explains why similar doctrinal formulations try to capture experiences that are not necessarily identical.

Summary

An almost inevitable conclusion is that while the religious beliefs of most people derive from doctrines carried by religious systems and groups, they can be as 'primitive' as any postulates in mathematics and science, or in the knowledge we use to cope more or less successfully with our environment. The validity of primitive beliefs is seldom questioned, since they are supported by self-fulfilling expectations and the authority of a social consensus. Therefore a believer's credibility depends less on holding particular beliefs than on some general orientation to what is to be believed.

To know that religious beliefs are coherently structured in terms of their content tells us nothing about how they are used. Believed truth, hoped-for truth, or a social consensus make up the 'objective knowledge' that supports morality or explains what is otherwise inexplicable because it is mysterious and beyond rational discussion, or at the frontier of scientific understanding. Some can balance the claims of science and religion by keeping them in separate domains, while others believe that trying to study how we come to terms with religion necessarily reduces and conflicts with the validity of any religious claims. These explanations certainly keep changing and there is more support and recognition now for social or cognitive theories of religion than for the earlier motivational or emotional explanations of it.

When religious believers account for their own beliefs, they confront the same problems and questions that face anyone who would make a psychological explanation. Do we have control over ourselves or is that located beyond each of us? Are beliefs tested by faithfulness or by action? How much knowledge do we need to be a committed believer? In what sense do we construct our own religion? Is the sacred a social category? Why is a belief in God still widespread, while belief in a life after death has declined? Why are more people putting themselves in the 'no religion' category? Why are there fewer Catholic/Protestant differences now? Why do cross-national comparisons of religious belief and practice show such great differences?

Most of the findings about religious belief rely on surveys and questionnaires that elicit controlled responses to slogan-like statements about the Devil, hell, heaven, God, or reincarnation. The beliefs that people hold are, however, far more subtle than questionnaires and their simplified issues allow. It may be for this reason that surveys have successfully exposed the links between religious belief and age, sex, and social class, but not with psychological measures. Surveys have emphasized the importance of contextual influences and the traditional interpretations that focus our religions on parental pressures, social prejudices and religious experience. But only in committed conversations about religion are strongly-held beliefs likely to be revealed: even when that happens they are too easily over-interpreted in psychological terms.

8 Experience and Mysticism

And he [Jacob] dreamed, and behold a ladder set up on the earth, and the top of it reached to heaven: and behold the angels of God ascending and descending on it.

Genesis 28.12

In the year that King Uzziah died I saw also the Lord sitting upon a throne, high and lifted up, and his train filled the temple.

Isaiah 6.1

Popular assumptions about the deeply hidden motives for 'being religious' imply that any appeal or claims to a religious experience can be explained with reference either to some underlying psychological reaction to stress or to social conditions that might induce such an experience, the influence of a particular place and the other people there and what they were doing. Since few non-religious people accept that religious experiences reflect valid insights into the nature of 'reality' they often explain them in terms of a need for security or consolation, a psychiatric illness, or with reference to the physiology of the brain. Drugs are widely known to evoke altered states of consciousness with emotional, sensual, and mystical overtones that might be like those that contemplatives have cultivated through their disciplined lives.

The intangibility and ambiguity of religious experience reflect not only the different ways they can be produced and their sanctions, but the language that is available to describe them. The basic information we have about religious experiences is found in rather stereotyped descriptions, almost all written from within a religious tradition. William James emphasized that 'Religious language clothes itself in such poor symbols as our life affords' (1985, p. 18). He commented on the 'amatory' or sexual symbols that are common among accounts of religious experiences, which also include references to eating and drinking, as in 'we hunger and thirst after righteousness', or 'taste and see that the Lord is good'. Such metaphors try to capture particular experiences that show others what they might be like. Objective measures of change in the electrical potential of the brain, cerebral blood flow or muscular relaxation are poor indices of any but the simplest mental events and certainly cannot identify whether a religious experience is genuine or not. William James argued that a genuine first-hand religious experience must be heterodox, and that when it defines some orthodoxy its 'day of inwardness is over'.

Work on 'altered states of consciousness' which has explored the effects of using a mantra, as in Transcendental Meditation (TM), and practising yogic exercises, show how some meditative practices produce changes in body image and in the sense of time, as well as other perceptual distortions and emotional changes that parallel psychotic states and may not always be benign. Social support is probably as important for these as for traditional western religious experiences, since here too we must learn what to expect and how to cope with it. Deliberately manipulated experiences are *probably* different from the rare religious experiences that occur spontaneously.

Our understanding of why some people are so skilful at describing their experiences is incomplete, and we do not know why we dream, search for beauty, believe in ghosts, build complex fantasies or write (and read) science fiction. We can be certain, however, that experiences are almost always conveyed by language and lie somewhere between brain functions and the social or communal traditions that recognize and sanction them.

Melancholy

An earlier but misplaced concreteness aligned both melancholy and conversion with guilt or social control, especially in regard to an individual's sexual life, as important features of religion in adolescence. But, as William James said, 'The plain truth is that to interpret religion one must in the end look at the immediate content of the religious consciousness' (ibid., p. 19). It is now recognized that this consciousness depends on the ways religious traditions are presented, and the solutions or models that are then entered into experience. As St Teresa of Avila wrote: 'One day, being in orison, it was granted me to perceive in one instant how all things are seen and contained in God.' On another occasion, when reciting the Athanasian Creed she said that 'Our Lord made me comprehend in what way it is that one God can be in Three Persons. He made me see it so clearly that I remained as extremely surprised as I was comforted' (quoted by William James, 1985, p. 326). Descriptions like these refer to intellectual and emotional (or cognitive and affective) reactions to material that has been presented from the outside. St John of the Cross in his *Dark Night of the Soul* explains how a given 'aridity' of soul may result from a stripping of the soul of its imperfections, from a frailty or lukewarmness of spirit, from an indisposition, or from a disorder of the 'humours' of the body.

Because the boundaries of our consciousness are blurred, we often need the advice or counsel of other people to interpret or test our own conclusions about what any experience might mean. Private insights may, like dreams, be hidden from view and only cautiously made public in the censored form we are prepared to tell others. Religion and its language for experience provides its own context within which that can be done. Religious theories of the world and of our place in it make full use of the natural metaphors of day and night, horizontal and vertical, life and death. Some reject such constructed views, preferring realist analyses or their own direct apprehension of the world. But any account of experience sets a scene that encloses inquiries about whatever might be implied with confident claims to valid experiences. While we can look beyond descriptions of those experiences to the insights they reveal and their consequences it is hard to know exactly what causes them.

While the classical argument from design is probably the most commonly accepted argument for the existence of God, when social scientists ask people what they believe about God they refer to personal processes that are usually beyond their awareness or to the dictates of social and cultural processes. Explanations of religious experience are similarly set between those poles, but rest on self-descriptions. Only the most committed cynic can dismiss someone's account of their experiences, although it is easier to reject the meanings that are assigned to them.

While dreamers are encouraged to befriend their dreams and psychotics their delusions, a defining feature of psychosis as a psychiatric disorder is the patients' lack of insight into the fact that their symptoms are abnormal, unusual and not shared with others. Patients who assert that they are possessed by another human being, or that they are God or Napoleon, have a delusion of reference strikingly different from a Christian sense of the presence of God. Direct claims to religious experience or insight are to be 'discerned' (or evaluated) on religious or other grounds, especially when they involve the ecstatic or insightful experiences of the primal reality William James believed to be the essence of religion, when he defined it as 'the feelings, acts and experiences of individual men in their solitude, so far as they stand in relation to whatever they may consider the divine' (1985, p. 31). While a religion might resolve the existential problems of discontented and solitary individuals, it does more than that by linking us with a tradition of hopeful interpretation.

A basic problem is whether the religious experiences and mystical states that can be induced by ascetic practices, prayer and contemplation, or in some other way, are autonomous 'gifts of the spirit', or involve an inherently psychological condition. Theologians and scientists inevitably disagree on the origins, meaning or consequences and the most appropriate means of studying such experiences. The variety of their forms range from physical sensations to 'intellectual visitations' and insights that cannot draw conviction directly.

Empirical studies

Several recent studies of religious experience have relied on answers to the late Sir Alister Hardy's question, 'Have you ever been aware of or influenced by a presence or a power, whether you call it God or not, which is different from your everyday self?' An obvious limitation to such data is an unwillingness to describe experiences that are by definition 'private', although David Hay (1982) argues that since different forms of the question yield similar results they all tap the same universe of discourse. He has found that 'between 30 and 40 per cent of British and American adults would certainly claim to have had an experience like this, at least once in their lives' (1982, p. 137), although a quarter of them had never spoken to anyone about that experience for fear of ridicule, or because they might be thought insane. Despite that, those who report having had mystical experiences have been found to score higher on measures of psychological competence (Hood, 1976), optimism (Greeley, 1974) and altruism (Wuthnow, 1978). This is, however, more likely to reflect the effects of these experiences than whatever might have caused them.

The use of experience therefore becomes a question about how they are to be displayed or talked about, while their credibility is more usually assessed with reference to the experiencer's own background than to the experience itself, since to interpret that would imply some gnostic superiority. A paradoxical aspect of the evidence that is accepted as a basis for religious insight is found in Back and Bourque's (1970) conclusion that what some people identify as a 'religious' experience others describe as aesthetic, or simply as having had a 'good time'. Identifying any experience involves fitting it into a socially recognized frame, and we are troubled when that cannot be done. In this sense, religion itself produces *and* resolves the experiences and feelings it sanctions.

While the power of religion to precipitate guilt, alienation, despondency and other emotions defies its personal and social relevance, these aspects of it have been neglected by psychologists but not by mystics and spiritual directors, especially within the Catholic traditions. It might even be that these traditions have only recently accepted the contributions that empirical psychology can make to the study of religion because of their concern with, and their expertise in, mystical experience and spiritual direction. While some psychologists still find it hard to handle conversion experiences in terms that are neither physiological nor behavioural, many now accept what seems to be the obvious fact that to describe an experience involves an attempt to systematize and control it, and even to persuade others to accept it. If someone with any kind of pain finds sympathy for it among strangers, they do so by tapping a collective wisdom (or consciousness) and the resulting companionship. It may be for this reason that established prayer groups and the recent move towards group-based and self-help therapies are so well able to instil confidence and provide effective support. The development of hospices is similarly helping to make dying a less ambiguous (or rejected) experience.

In part, these movements aim to restore some aspects of social life that have been removed by our mobile and urban-based modern life-styles, with some people hoping to give churches a greater role in local communities. Anticipating death is another important but until recently neglected feature of the psychology of religion despite the continuing and widespread belief that one of the 'reasons' for religion itself is to provide hope in the face of death, and to cope with that and the other unpredictable features of life. The Prayer Book therefore asks for us to be delivered 'from lightning and tempest; from plague, pestilence, and famine; from battle and murder, and from sudden death'.

About three-quarters of national samples in the United States (but only 45 per cent in Britain) believe in a life after death. An inconsistency is shown in Britain, where 57 per cent believe in heaven (compared with 68 per cent in the United States) and 54 per cent believe in hell. That slightly more among older people believe in an afterlife does not necessarily show the effects of age itself on that belief, since it was probably more widespread when they were young than it is now. Premonitions of death, near-death experiences and out of the body experiences are often given as supporting evidence for those beliefs, although cultural influences have paramount effects on that content. Eastern traditions have far more tolerance of these mystical or supernatural happenings than is the case in the western world.

The research directed specifically at deciding how positive attitudes to death align with religious belief is equivocal because of the complexity of those attitudes and their relationships. Spilka et al., (1985, pp. 131f) have discussed these problems, which include specifying the aspects of death most closely related to particular religious orientations or perspectives, as well as the spiritual possibilities and confidence expressed. As with many other religious phenomena, the evidence most people accept is anecdotal or descriptive. Despite the problems in confidently establishing general relationships, Christian belief and ministry is firmly oriented towards death, to those who mourn and the moral issues involved. The clergy, who are typically the ones who carry religion to those who are dying, characteristically offer to pray for or with them. Spilka et al. conclude, however, that 'much of the available research on religion and death is questionable because of a failure to appreciate the intricacies of how humans link their feelings about death to the personal theology they hold, and how the latter is further connected to the religio-social order' (p. 151) by their beliefs in 'a benevolent after-life'. It is likely that one's own experience is another important component of this. If these attitudes *are* influenced by wishes and hopes that are not well-articulated, they involve the oldest problems religion has dealt with, which still focus our thoughts on religious matters. Whether life itself is a source of anxiety depends on one's orientation or state of mind, and on whether an emphasis is placed on our deficiencies or the growth that religion might help us achieve.

A changed focus

A striking development in psychology has been its recent focus on cognitive processes, consciousness, states of mind and the awareness of self. Automatic actions, information processing and memory, the cerebral localization of pyschological functions, paradoxical experiences, and the effects of meditation and drugs are all being fitted into those perspectives. Yet the traditional approaches through self-reported or phenomenological accounts have not been replaced, beyond recognizing that no introspective account is simply read-out from an internal 'screen' of feelings or memories of what has been 'seen'.

Religious experiences have therefore been variously interpreted as irrelevant, aberrant and anomalous, a consequence of deprivation or of over-stimulation and arousal, the result of an external event or as an extraordinary insight into the nature of reality or of 'the Holy'. This sense of the numinous has biblical and traditional sanctions that may be simply accepted or deconstructed. To accept them as more than rhetorical conceits or mistaken interpretations demands the eye of faith. So what *did* St Teresa of Avila mean when, in her dream of an angel, she saw,

In his hands a long golden spear and at the end of the iron tip I seemed to see a point of fire. With this he seemed to pierce my heart repeatedly so that it penetrated to my entrails. When he drew it out I thought he was drawing them out with it and he left me completely afire with a great love of God. The pain was so great that I screamed aloud, but simultaneously felt such an infinite sweetness that I wished the pain would last eternally.

When anyone makes their dreams public, we become involved with them (and it is more common in some other cultures to describe your dreams than it is in ours). The language we use to do that seems to be detached. Older psychological assumptions which have interpreted the content of dreams directly, with a focus by turns on what they convey about our inward or outward worlds, emphasize the inherently ambiguous dualism of dreams and religious experiences.

Numerous theories have explained the enlightenment that follows from deliberately inculcated or inadvertent experiences that can produce a sense of awe, especially when it is directed towards God. The tension between our desire (with a parallel sense of debt) and the constraints imposed by physical and social realities are resolved differently by each religious tradition and the individuals within them.

Despite efforts over the last fifteen years to escape from the constraints of questionnaire procedures, with assessments of experience through physiological or reaction time measures of arousal, little progress has been made apart from finding that meditation directed specifically to relaxation or an altered consciousness does have positive effects on those who persevere with it. This could, however, involve a placebo effect and not a direct consequence of whatever self-control might be developed. Those approaches have not yet been brought to the centre of an explicit psychology of religion. Even if they were, we would still have to examine the way people talk about experiences and how they avoid being misunderstood, especially when an inner life of fantasy and imagination (with its 'as if' statements) is contrasted with action. Some cultures or traditions keep experience alive, while others try to reduce that inner life to an infantile dependency or an intellectual game. In that sense religious experience fills a space between the institutional perspectives on a religion that is to be used, and a direct, personally experienced (or rejected) sense of God.

Summary

Schachter and Singer's (1962) two-factor theory of emotion emphasized that we constantly use (and look for) situational cues about how others are reacting when we identify states of emotional arousal, like those involving fear or awe. When John Donne said that 'No man is an island . . .' he helped to replace strictly personal or functional meanings by the necessity of society. Yet claims to personal experience are still accepted as evidence, and not only as a rhetorical device that applies to particular reference systems. To claim some experience is therefore stronger than saying, 'I believe in . . .'. William James argued that, 'To pass a judgment upon these states, we must not content ourselves with superficial medical talk, we must inquire into their "fruits for life"', which he said, 'appear to have been various' (1985, p. 327). The gaps between experience and the telling about it are filled by potent symbols that are neither theologically nor psychologically neutral, since they involve commitment to a truth that has been experienced for oneself, which can also be judged by others as illusory.

9 Religious Development and Christian Education

When I was a child, I spake as a child, I understood as a child, I thought as a child.

1 Corinthians 13.11

In the late nineteenth century, studies of religious development were based on broadly evolutionary assumptions that looked equally to the religious psychology of childhood and to anthropological studies of 'primitive' groups to answer questions about the intellectual and social origins of religion. Two important, if oppressive conclusions from those studies were that religion had indeed 'developed', and that Christianity was the culmination of that development. There is now, however, a respect for the complexity of religious phenomena, and the realization that whatever values and 'natural progressions' might have been detected could have been constructed or imposed by the investigators themselves. This applies to studies among western children as much as to the study of religion in non-Christian societies, which operate within social orders having their own authenticity. Those traditions may or may not be accepted by adults in our own society. It is of some interest, however, that the *Journal for the Scientific Study of Religion* has not yet published a paper on religious development, despite the fact that during its early period in the 1960s Piaget's theories were so dominant.

Psychological development is however no longer formulated within a single explanatory framework, and the focus of studies of religious development has moved from conversion to the child's 'natural' knowledge or understanding of the world. This move was greatly influenced by Piaget's theory of an intellectual progression from concrete representations to formal, abstract, or logical operations. More recently that development has been focused on moral judgement by Kohlberg (Munsey, 1980) and then on the stages in the development of faith by James Fowler (Dykstra and Parks, 1986; Webster, 1984). The methods that have been used to validate each of those approaches use the answers to controlled questions to test for the expected sequence of stages through which religious thinking develops towards a 'mature' perspective (the features of which must be carefully specified). Developmental psychologists have also looked at

95

changes in the ideas of God, religious attitudes and the effects of religion itself (Strommen, 1971). While most of this work has been presented as if it were theoretically open and inductive, it is often driven by implicit assumptions about what children (in particular) are capable of, or can be expected to do at any age or stage.

There are very few behavioural experiments in the manner of Hartshorne and May (1928), who studied the honesty of children by allowing them to cheat when they marked their own answers to an arithmetic test. When their cheating was later related to their church-going, no clear association was found, although children who had attended Sunday school were the least likely to have been 'honest'. (In these experiments, Hartshorne and May themselves cheated their children to get the data they needed, by comparing a carbon copy of the original answers with alterations the children made as they marked their own work.) Derek Wright (1971) noted in this context that although a religious training does not make one resist temptation, it can intensify guilt. It also helps one give socially desirable answers, although when it is believed that immoral actions might be detected by others, religiousness has a restraining effect. Crandall and Gozali (1969) reported a similar conclusion, based on data from a question-naire measuring socially desirable answers, finding that US and Swedish Catholic and Lutheran children gave significantly more 'desirable' responses (agreeing that 'When I make a mistake, I always admit I am wrong' and 'Sometimes I do things I've been told not to do') than did children at (non-denominational) state schools.

An alternative to this view of deliberately planned action is the spontaneous religion children are thought to show in their ready beliefs about God, which could reflect what adults tell their children about the origin and nature of the world. In that sense, parents form a coalition with God's authority by which they try to control and forestall the independence of their children. A few cynics argue that all religious explanations are primarily suited to children anyway.

Intellectual development

Piaget's open-ended method of questioning children about their religious (and other) beliefs has supported these differences between our 'spontaneous' and our 'acquired' or traditional responses to religion, and between the 'ego-centric' and later decentred cognitions or perspectives, especially about concepts of God, prayer and religious identity. Clear stages have been identified in that material.

Harms (1944) found that an early fairy-tale stage was followed by a realistic (or 'human') stage and then an individualistic or imaginative stage in drawings of God that children had been asked to make. Deconchy (1967) identified attributive, personalized and then interiorized themes in the words that children aged between eight and sixteen associated with the concept of 'God'. Long, Elkind and Spilka's (1967) study of prayer found that after about age seven, formulaic prayers were replaced by concretely self-oriented prayers, and that around eleven children's prayers became more abstract and decentred. Elkind (1963) similarly found that answers to questions about religious denominations such as, 'Is your family Catholic (or Jewish)?', 'How do you become a Catholic?', and, 'How can you tell whether a person is a Catholic?', followed the same trend towards greater abstraction and differentiation. Goldman's (1964) study of children's understanding of the meaning of Bible stories and pictures, which retrieved Piaget's stages of thinking with an intuitive (or guessing) stage around seven or eight, followed by concrete interpretations, and then a formal or abstract stage at about thirteen or fourteen, found immediate acceptance among religious educators, who then used it as a basis for writing new curricula.

The developmental stages in thinking and problem solving that Piaget identified shaped the thinking of teachers and parents about their children as much as Dr Spock's (1955) book on baby and child-care did. Despite that influence, recent criticisms have made both approaches rather unfashionable. It is now not only agreed that any set of 'stages' may be a fictional construction, but that children seldom give truly spontaneous answers when adults ask them questions that are tailored to what children are expected to know, or will talk about to adults. Too little research has pursued the implications of the realization that childhood is divided between the adults' focus on it (and their own memories about it) and the autonomous world of childhood itself.

Moral development

These problems are nowhere more evident than in Kohlberg's theory of moral development, first published in the 1960s and still being discussed because of its prescriptive nature and reliance on the specific theory of justice advanced by John Rawls (cf. Colby and Kohlberg, 1987). But Kohlberg himself emphasized that a scientific study of morality cannot be ethically neutral. The stages of moral development that Kohlberg identified move from a preconventional dependence on immediate and obvious consequences, to a conventional dependence on social approval, to an autonomous, principled level that defines moral values in terms of a recognized legal or social contract and finally to a dependence on universal ethical principles. Data to support this analysis were derived from lengthy discussions about the ways in which moral dilemmas should be resolved. James Fowler's (1981) now fashionable theory of 'faith development' broadened Kohlberg's stages of moral development. He identified six stages: an intuitive-projective faith, a mythic-literal faith, a synthetic-conventional faith, an inductive-reflective faith, a paradoxical-consolidative faith, and finally a universalizing faith. He regards these stages as designations for a way of 'leaning into life' or making sense of one's existence where faith involves a 'life-wager'.

Kohlberg's and Fowler's theories have been easily criticized for their prescriptiveness. The controversies that have been developed centre on them as sets of rules that articulate what parents or teachers think a mature religiousness should be. Criticism of this work includes Carol Gilligan's (1982) *In a Different Voice*. She questioned the implicitly male perspective in the work on moral development which assumes that the meanings men identify or impose on moral and other dilemmas offer the best solutions. She supports her analysis with women's arguments to resolve the moral dilemmas that Kohlberg used, for example, 'Is it morally justified for a husband to steal a drug that would save his wife's life?' and those that women give who have actually asked for an abortion. Gilligan has found that it is typical for women to cast those dilemmas not as a contest of rights but as problems of relationships that centre on questions of responsibility (p. 59). As she says, 'The elusive mystery of women's development lies in its recognition of the continuing importance of attachment in the human life cycle. Woman's place in man's life cycle is to protect this recognition while the developmental litany intones the celebration of separation, autonomy, individuation and natural rights' (p. 23). She concludes that for Kohlberg to identify the highest stage of moral development with a concept of rights generalizes a male perspective that makes women feel 'excluded from direct participation in society, [so that] they see themselves as subject to a consensus of judgement made and enforced by the men on whose protection and support they depend and by whose names they are known' (p. 67).

A similar criticism can be made against the male authority of the church, clergy and revealed texts. Some claim that their unyielding and hierarchical authority gives inadequate answers to the wrong questions, and does not confront the issues of exploitation and hurt that had troubled Erikson (1969) as he was writing about Gandhi's life. Erikson found a contradiction between Gandhi's non-violence when dealing with the British and the psychologically violent ways he dealt with his family and the children in the ashram, and wrote of 'the presence of a kind of untruth in the very protestation of truth; of something unclear when all the words spelled out an unreal purity; and, above all, of displaced violence when non-violence was the professed issue' (p. 231).

That problem does not relate specifically to maleness or femaleness, although its focus there is easily explained in terms of an inherently nurturing and interactive role which makes (many) girls experience themselves as being like their mothers, thereby fusing their experience of attachment with their identity, while boys (at least in most Western societies), in separating themselves from their mothers develop a more emphatic sense of self. A consequence of this is that moral problems arise 'from conflicting responsibilities rather than from competing rights and requires for its resolution a mode of thinking that is contextual and narrative rather than formal and abstract' (Gilligan, 1982, p. 19). This argument has a clear relevance to the dilemmas that many women, and some men as well, feel that Christianity confronts them with when it offers a hierarchical system rather than a web of relationships, and applies its own religious sanctions to resolve criticism of those problems.

While these moral theories have allowed some constructive interpretations, they are not yet well-founded empirically, and need to be more carefully tested. Furthermore, any set of developmental stages implies some process of 'maturation', yet experience is needed before anybody can move to the next stage or display new skills as they solve problems in defined contexts. Each new stage displays a competence that may have been masked when earlier skills are no longer appropriate, although relationships, especially between a child (as subject) and an adult (as either a male or female questioner) will itself obscure what can be expressed. Children's interactions with adults and with strangers are limited by what they are either expected or allowed to say. It is more important to let people use their own terms to describe their experiences and conclusions about life.

Despite those social and psychological constraints, children achieve an adult linguistic capacity by about the age of five, which suggests that they do not *have* to go on acting like children, except when they are not allowed to participate in adult society (for example, by not being admitted to Communion) or do not have the strength or other competencies to do so. Confirmation marks a social transition that does not actually require a particular ability or even knowledge of the catechism, a personal choice, decision, or commitment beyond what that context itself prescribes. This rite does, however, sanction an opportunity to practise what is required by a set of social rules that specify whatever it is that those who have been confirmed *can* do.

If the criteria for a mature religiousness could be made quite explicit, we might all know what to say or do that would show our maturity. But it is not just children who appear immature because they have not been given the training, since adults also recognize that among the different ways of being religious some are more 'natural' or spontaneous than others and do not need to be deliberately cultivated. But if, following Fowler, the most mature form of religion involves 'images and energies from a deeper self ', rather than holding to a set of impersonal attributes for God, there seems no reason for not explicitly stating that it *is* possible to act or talk in this way. One problem, of course, is that such formulations are not universally agreed, and that the simpler, more direct forms of faith are still admired.

It has even been argued that 'childhood' (as a set of stages) was invented comparatively recently, and that it is the fact that children *look* young which confuses assessments and expectations about their intellectual development or maturity. Young children *can* make sensible generalizations, and they show a good sense of order and of the rightness or fairness of things if they are given opportunities to display those skills and have their understanding checked by a sympathetic adult. Peter Lawrence (1965) showed this by asking parents who were involved with a church to record their own children's *spontaneous* questions. He found that most of these questions were *doctrinal*, and concerned the nature of the deity, suffering and death, churches and the Word, and manifestations of the supernatural. No questions about everyday morality were recorded.

Childhood and later

Lawrence concluded that religious educators must recognize the importance of giving children specific *and* correct (or rather, adult) instances of abstract principles, rather than restricting them to childish examples. We find out more about children (and other adults) by listening to them than by questioning them, and need not force what we hear into *our* rigid categories. Concrete and abstract forms of thinking are, like the contrast between animistic (or child-like) and 'scientific' forms of thought, inevitably intertwined by adults and probably among children too. That eight-year-olds give more confident explanations of simple scientific phenomena (like why drops of water form on the outside of a glass full of water) than fourteen-year-olds who have been taught some science emphasizes that science is typically dealt with in a way that shatters their implicit understanding. Religious educators may have similarly rigid expectations about what those they teach should understand, which is often too concrete because they assume that their pupils are immature. But given the opportunity, children readily tell you when they don't understand. Teachers also forget that the 'edges' of doctrine are often blurred among adults whose 'religious knowledge' is vestigial. Theologians have more information than most adults, who know more than their children. Yet theologians, with their sophisticated perspectives, have plenty of room for disagreement, since even the simplest issues of faith can be easily questioned and turned into issues for re-negotiation; this can, however, threaten the standing of those who appear to be orthodox (cf. Bowker, 1987).

That young people reject what they are offered in the name of 'religion' is shown by Francis and Carter's (1980) studies of attitudes to religion among young people in Church of England, Roman Catholic and Local Authority schools. No differences were found in pupil attitudes in the separate groups of schools, and they concluded that the 'findings provide no support for the notion that church-sponsored secondary schools exert a positive influence on their pupils' attitudes to religion'. In a further analysis, the parents' religious behaviour was found to have a correlation of +.49 with their child's religious behaviour, which in turn had a correlation of +.54 with the child's attitude to religion. That was the only significant finding in their analysis of positive religious attitudes. The effects of what is expected in the social world of school accounts for these results better than any evidence about the intellectual or cognitive development of these pupils.

We have already noted that the very early research on adolescent religion centred on the changes in belief that surround a conversion experience or decision, and on the problems of ensuring good behaviour. Against that interest is a clear trend for those between the ages of twelve and eighteen to express increasing disbelief about traditional doctrines. It is not clear if this simply reflects their move towards independence, the greater accountability expected of them by adults, their flirtation with new beliefs, or a 'true' decrease in religiousness. Those questions cannot be resolved without subtle measures and long-term studies of the same people. Conclusions drawn from cross-sectional studies of changes in belief among those of different ages to identify age-related trends are confounded by changes in their social contexts. Those who are now eighty, for example, grew up when religion was more firmly established than it appears to have become, and their apparently stronger beliefs may reflect that more than anything about the beliefs of elderly people. It is therefore unreasonable to conclude that people become more religious as they age, or even that religious believers live longer.

Godin's developmental tasks

André Godin's guide to understanding the tasks that might be involved in a developing awareness of religion aimed to integrate dynamic (or Freudian) perspectives with developmental psychology and with Christian thought, on the assumption that we must be taught not only 'what is to be believed' but 'how to believe'. His goal was to achieve a decentred, sacramental religiousness that is not naively magical or superstitious, yet has a personal perspective. Godin (1971) therefore identified five tasks for Christian education.

The first involves awakening an historical awareness of God's plan in history. Beginning with stories that enliven the imagination, he advocated using them as a frame on which to hang one's own surprising experiences. Those experiences then revive and interpret the historical context, attaching value and a sense of continuity to specific historical events.

The second task involves 'coming to see certain events as *signs* of God's action' (p. 123) in the relationships between material events and their spiritual meanings, and then distinguishing between reality and symbolically significant myths about it.

Godin's third task involves transforming magical attitudes into a sacramental perspective. That developments task is especially important for belief about the efficacy of petitionary prayer. Thouless and Brown (1964), for example, found a decreasing belief from ages twelve to seventeen in the material effectiveness of such prayers, with few differences between people in the different denominations. There were, however, pronounced denominational differences in what it was thought appropriate to pray for, with Methodists but not Catholics disapproving of praying that a horse might win a race. Those data emphasize aspects of religious teaching that are neglected by those more committed to indoctrination than to conveying a religious orientation to the meaning of Bible narratives, the gospel, and the practice of religion.

Godin's fourth task involves a 'progressive reduction of moralism', with a conscience that is neither punitive nor based simply on confusing morality with Christianity. He found a theological solution to that problem in Christian hope and in the 'final justification on the basis of God's pardon in Jesus Christ' (p. 136). That perspective would replace moral imperatives by putting the intentionality of actions into a religious context. An extrinsic religious attitude that would resolve the burden of guilt through an individual wishfulness must also be transformed into a transcendentally 'religious' perspective. A religion that is expected to produce miracles can easily be discarded when it fails (even though such failure might be explained away).

The fifth task is to purify our images of God, which involves reconstructing traditional symbols, as *pointers* to order and meaning within some larger structure.

Erik Erikson (1974) identified the contrast between integrity and despair as the most adult phase in a developmental sequence that moved through basic trust, autonomy, initiative (rather than guilt), industry, identity and intimacy, to generativity. That these endpoints have been identified in principle stresses the importance of a guiding theory to interpret results that can also structure our understanding of what might be involved in developing a specifically religious perspective.

Schneider and Dornbusch (1950), who analysed forty-six best-selling inspirational books published in America after 1875, emphasized that a religion which satisfies the desire for consolation, power, and success can protect our socially desirable values. John A. T. Robinson (1963) similarly stressed that many people continue to teach what they have ceased to believe for themselves. A God who might restore a lost Paradise is often presented in a way that can never challenge whatever is offered. For Godin (1971, p. 149) therefore, 'the *criterion* of a Christian maturity is the distance it maintains from the psychological traits of a purely human religiosity'.

It is unfortunate that most of the work that has been referred to here derives from the 1960s. There is too little recent material that can be cited, and the problems identified in the 1960s remain, as does the tone (and the drone) of a moralistic and oppressive teaching that disregards the ambiguity of illusions and the realities in religion, especially as we either encounter our own projected wishes *or* the Other, and face the facts of life and death either inside or beyond a religious faith.

Religion is not usually taught in a way that challenges existing beliefs in an open-ended dialogue, but in a manner that hopes to develop a defined religious attachment and identity. (Studies of religious attitudes and beliefs have been similarly convergent.) If the goals of any religious training are to be evaluated, and not just taken on trust, they should be expressed in a way that allows any effects to be measured. The specific context in which a religion is expressed will, however, impose its limitations on what is tolerated or allowed, and on what is required of our understanding in meeting religious obligations and practice.

Summary

Questions about religious education and the development of a mature form of religion must be read against changes over the last thirty years in the aims, contexts and content of religious education, whether at home, at church or in school. Many state schools have now replaced religious education by moral education or courses in personal development, and most recently by a focus on peace and justice. Attempts during the 1960s to identify the psychological principles that might guide teaching practice and the curriculum are now criticized for their unduly principled perspective, and the absence of supporting or evaluative research. Yet they could (and should) have been evaluated. The effects of any theoretically-sound conception that is applied in practice should be assessed, whether in the believed efficacy of prayer, orientations to religion or the attitudes of teachers. Despite the attention that has been given to school- or church-based religious education, parental attitudes to religion have been found to have a far more potent influence on young adults' involvements with religion.

'Readiness for religion', or for any other aspect of life, depends on what is expected rather than on innate intellectual (or physical) characteristics, although a child-like openness and wonder about the natural (and social) order may be as necessary for coming to terms with religion as it is for developing a scientific perspective. No *single* approach has clarified the intellectual or emotional origins of either science or religion. Yet both are received (and valued) aspects of our culture, and are shaped by their own doctrines and social control.

Since developmental psychologists neglected religion in favour of studies of basic psychological processes like learning, perception and adaptation, educational research has concentrated on language, mathematics, and the opportunities school systems seem to disallow because of their 'hidden curricula'. Understanding the effectiveness of any schooling requires that attention is given to the language and the concepts required of those who are being judged for their competence, whatever their age. To solve those problems requires teamwork and patient inquiry. Finding how it is that we learn to deal competently with religion might therefore be more important than trying to identify what we are expected to know about it.

10 Theoretical Problems in the Psychology of Religion

We are all here using the word 'death', which is a public instrument, which has a whole technique [of usage]. Then someone says he has an idea of death. . . . If you treat this [idea] as something private, with what right are you calling it an idea of death?

L. Wittgenstein, *Lectures on Religious Belief*, 1966, p. 69

Our aim so far has been to show how modern psychology deals with religion. A great deal more could have been mentioned by citing and commenting on specific studies and examining in detail the basic psychological and social principles that are used to understand religion in terms of social learning or influence, and how we make sense of our experiences, hopes and fears. We could have explicitly contrasted the polemical views of anti-religionists (who believe that religion is an unqualified mistake) against those who assert that religion is the only force for good.

Although theologians appeal to the 'evidence', many people cannot allow the social sciences to arbitrate on religious questions, even when they ask whether there might be social and psychological differences between those who are or are not religious, or why some religious groups enforce more compliance with their doctrines and practices than others. Answers to those questions often appear inconsistent and even paradoxical because, while some religious people are less humanitarian, more bigoted and more anxious than those who are not religious, other religious people are enabled by their religion to work against social and religious prejudices. Non-religious people can also be intolerant and arrogant towards those who disagree with them.

While any findings are limited by the size of the groups that have been studied and by the validity of the assumptions underlying whatever measures have been taken, it is hard to conclude that religion *alone* has formed anyone's view of the world or their personality, since it does not work in isolation from the other social processes within which it is embedded.

The simplest conclusion we can draw is that while it is unsafe to make categorical or universal statements about the consequences of adopting any religious stance, a psychological perspective helps to clarify the over-simplified conclusions that many people seem pleased to reach for. The implicitly psychological assumptions that often support judgements about religious perspectives or people must be questioned, especially when they refer to the 'unconscious needs' religion 'satisfies' or to the 'types' of people who are attracted to religion. Such assumptions are hard to validate. Current psychology refers to those judgements as the attributions that are part of our search for the meaning we must find as we make sense of the world and of our place in it. Religious explanations are themselves a part of that search.

What must now be called the 'old' psychology of religion interpreted action in wilful or deliberate terms, or with reference to unconscious processes that are beyond the individual's awareness (and control) but which were identified by observers. Examples of such analyses refer to the 'compensations' or 'projections' involved in religion, as religious people were described as 'neurotic' or 'obsessional'. They identified religion as a 'natural response', an instinct or habit, and as defensive, protective and self-serving rather than challenging or constructive.

'Commonsense' tends to be aligned with that old psychology, supporting its explanations of religious phenomena with weak anecdotal evidence. But it is easier to find simple explanations that can answer our 'Why?' questions about both religious and non-religious people than it is to test those explanations or theories against replicable data that are not simply autobiographical. We should try to avoid making gratuitous interpretations of others' actions or offering rhetorical warnings about the dangers of becoming embroiled in religion. Such warnings are too often circular and self-fulfilling.

That 'old' psychology was developed within Christian contexts that carried their own religious injunctions and interpretations of behaviour, and referred more often to individual than to social processes, and assumed that a natural state or law governed relationships between the body (which was sinful) and the mind (cf. Romans 7.23).

The newer psychology of religion that has become current relies on sound measurement and looks to the results of carefully designed experiments that use objective measures of behaviour, as in the study of how the story of the Good Samaritan might influence behaviour we discussed in Chapter Three.

Experiments on the consequences of a religious perspective or context usually set out to control the conditions under which precise observations can be made and indirectly invite the participants to commit themselves to a specific course of action. The results from such experiments are much stronger than those from questionnaire studies in which people are asked to *say* what they might do, because of their precise control over the variables that are being manipulated or controlled. Since questionnaires are easily answered in ways that fit with what it is socially desirable to say, they are considered rather 'subjective' by many psychologists. Despite that, well-designed questionnaires do give data that are more reliable than our uncontrolled impressions. The element of deception implicit in nearly all psychological experiments is a special problem for those who think it unethical to introduce any control over other people. Even in a research context where the people being studied are not told what to expect, their responses can be deliberately shaped, and psychological 'experiments' have come to be distrusted by many people who expect psychologists to use some deception.

The problem here is essentially one of who will be in control of the answers being given as the data are collected. Discrepancies between what people actually do, what they are expected to do, what they will agree to do or will say they would do present important problems for anyone who wants to study the constraints on our behaviour, including the effects or consequences of a religious perspective. Pressures to conform to the demands of social reality may be as hard to resist (or control) as are the strident biological demands we are expected to tame and subdue. These strictly practical questions about the consequences of a religion are different from the problems that face those studying what people believe, or how they find meaning in the doctrines and ideas that are presented to them, since that information must be given deliberately.

Beyond whatever we may do and how we talk about, describe or justify our actions, lie the reasons attributed to them or found in them by the actors themselves and by other people. The emphasis that is given to particular meanings is necessarily framed within language. While going to church can be described piously ('to worship') or expediently ('to meet people'), explaining the actions of other people seems easier than explaining oneself. But conclusions about others' intentions are likely to be wrong, and we are most likely to account for our own actions with reference to situational demands, saying, for example, 'I had to do it because he was going to hit me'. Observers, with their external perspective, typically assume that people act consistently because of stable personality traits, saying that 'He always gets angry when he thinks he is threatened', or 'He is a religious person'. Explanations like these draw on psychological, religious, social and other assumptions about the reasons for action. But whose perspective is more accurate? This is an important question, especially when conclusions are drawn that would discount insight, experience or a sense of authenticity. It is also a reason for collecting systematic data that can test our conclusions.

The best psychological theories about personal or social action offer a conceptual structure that is testable, and make a particular phenomenon more intelligible. We seldom assume that all the actions of other people are simply habitual or automatic, partly because that is not interesting enough and partly because we expect that others are well-motivated anyway. We can, however, only test for that by looking for what people say about their goals, or by what we think of what they are 'really' doing. Interpretations in terms of our 'unconscious' or other drives or purposes are given about things we might have forgotten, or for which we have not yet found explanations. Since these psychological explanations span biological, experiential, social or interpersonal, and cultural or traditional influences, psychologists are not the only experts on behaviour.

Psychology in religion

Psychological explanations are not like the scientific accounts that help us to control or predict future events, but they can challenge or support the advice that is given so readily by those who believe they have found 'the key to happiness', a correct life-style, or a true path that all should follow. The innumerable options and pieces of advice that are offered are supported by a variety of opinions and doctrines (not necessarily religious) and by practices extending beyond meditation and relaxation to assertiveness training, stress management and dietary programmes. These options are readily accepted, or dismissed as fads.

Those who try to advise others or who testify to what has 'saved' them appeal to their own experience or judgement, to reason, to an outside authority, or to some social consensus for support. But even judgements about physical reality can be biased, and it can be hard to find evidence that will convince others about the credibility of one's own beliefs, whether they are about science, religion or how to live one's life.

Religious people typically claim their own direct or irreducible experiences of the sacred as evidence for something beyond or other than the prosaic and everyday world to sustain them through their breaking-points. To argue that it is illusory to have such direct insight or to believe the world is fundamentally benign draws on other sets of assumptions that have themselves been socially sanctioned.

The effectiveness or plausibility of a religion can be tested against the way it deals with crisis, the support it gives, or the coherence and structure it offers to life. While firm religious believers accept some 'truths', when those beliefs were developing they were being influenced by other people, and were not directly driven by personality-based preferences or traits such as dogmatism or conservatism. That believers submit, with varying degrees of conformity or commitment, to the authority of a religious group is independent of the specific content of the religious beliefs they have accepted. Deconchy (1980) has shown that such social processes control not only what is to be defined as 'religious', but the deviations that are tolerated from a norm. Those who go too far away from what is acceptable are soon put under pressure to conform, at least in public, unless they decide (or are forced) to defect from it.

Similar pressures towards conformity apply to those doing scientific research; and religious groups have often tried to neutralize the empirical findings they disapprove of (as in the arguments about evolution or special creation). One way to do that is to restrict the rights of others to carry out research or have access to research material. The systematic selection of information so that it will not question the ideological or social legitimacy of an established institutional system is found in science as well as in religion, and in medicine, politics, or wherever individuals interact as producers or consumers of a group's 'goods'. In this sense even religious control is limited by what the members will tolerate. Demands for liturgical reform or for a different role for women in the Church are current examples of these complex pressures for change. In a similar way, psychology, sociology and anthropology, as well as theology, have shaped those aspects of religion that it is 'possible' for us to examine.

Just as we cannot entirely disregard the nature of people and their relation to religion, a few religious concerns have influenced psychology. This is especially obvious with the early psychologists like Wundt and Freud. Later psychologists, especially Piaget, were concerned with the similarities between a child's mental life and an adult's religion, and the transformations that are needed to produce mature religious perspectives. If one takes as an example the ways a religious perspective can support or conflict with political activities in our everyday life, it is as easy to retreat into religion as into any other sanctuary, and religion can be used to justify conflicts with secular authorities. On the other hand religious ideals can also reconcile conflict or focus loyalty on a leader or nation.

Social psychologists and to a lesser extent personality psychologists have investigated religious groups and individuals for what they can reveal about the nature of group pressure, altruism and reduced dissonance. It should also be remembered that conversion experiences and religious belief have been used as analytic models for other attitudes and beliefs. In all this work we cannot afford to be doctrinaire about either our psychology or the religious perspectives that are adopted.

The contexts for religion are defined by institutional claims on the lives of believers; but very few who have been changed by a religion can in their turn alter the institutions that have influenced them.

The argument that some religious doctrines (like the belief in God as Father) have an inherent appeal to some types of people is hard to test properly, since it confounds religious training and what religions offer with any psychological needs that might be identified. It is also hard to establish what makes a belief in, say, life after death grow stronger or weaker. Even disregarding the fact that the evidence from survey data is often unreliable, it is impossible to trace the effects of changes in the religious and the social context on this or any other religious belief except in the broadest terms. It is, furthermore, likely that any effects of religion on the majority of people are only indirect, since comparatively few will find religious claims so pressing that they *must* structure their lives within the Church.

Most Christians accept their religion because they have grown up with it. To have been converted later, or to be 'twice-born' as William James put it, does not eliminate the conflict and confusion that surrounds life within any religious institution, except for those who have completely given up their independence. It is also impossible to predict *who* will be captured by religion. This reduces the value of psychological assessments of potential ordinands, except to help screen out those who may be psychiatrically disturbed. A fashion of the 1960s for a psychological screening of candidates for the ministry has been replaced by a cautious dependence on routine information about academic, social, and religious background and commitment, relying on that to assess the credibility of the candidates' own accounts of their involvement with the Church and their sense of vocation.

Many psychological questions about worship and prayer confront a similar tension between the most plausible interpretations. Although worship and prayer involve traditional practices and public control, the symbolic order that is carried by the meanings of what is said and done there needs to be understood, since the participants will have their own idiosyncratic interpretations of whatever they are doing. Questions of intention are not beyond the reach of the methods of psychology, although we must recognize that religion is a social activity, except for those who are completely out of touch with that reality. Symbols are then stretched too far or left too concrete and become mere counters with little intrinsic meaning, and in danger of over-interpretation.

A mature religion

Gordon Allport (1950) emphasized that we must guard against over-estimating the consistency or completeness of a mature religious perspective. He also identified mature religion as both differentiated and complex, subtle and highly personal, dynamic but motivationally autonomous, and detached from any instrumental self-justifications from which comfort and solace could be derived. As he said, 'religion should be less of a servant and more of a master in the economy of life' (ibid. p. 63), as it pervasively transforms one's life. A mature religion is therefore not fanatical but 'ordinarily fashioned in the workshop of doubt' (p. 73), so that its 'beneficent consequences slowly strengthen the faith and cause the movements of doubt gradually to disappear' (p. 74). Since religion does not answer scientific questions, its beliefs are to be held tentatively, like 'working hypotheses', which recognize that others will not necessarily agree with them, as one becomes 'sure without being cocksure'. That we will still be alive tomorrow is a good (and optimistic) hypothesis which contrasts with the more stringent view that we should live each day as if it were our last. When 'religion' defines a path and not the barriers, it implies commitment without a complete set of rules or prescriptions for action, since the 'letter' soon kills.

A more external attitude to religion distinguishes the institutional demands on roles, positions or offices from the characteristics of those who occupy them. This approach has been developed by Scandinavian psychologists of religion who have identified mystical or ecstatic and other rituals performed by religious specialists in terms of the ways they correspond with local or cultural expectations of what religion should do. Sundén (1974) argued that this separation is possible *because* our intentions (and experiences) are structured or interpreted with social roles and functions that are themselves derived from, and sanctioned by, religious traditions, through the roles that embody 'God–man' or spirit–people relationships in myths and rites.

This view of religiousness recognizes alignments between social traditions and the demands that structure our awareness and understanding in such a way that experiences can take (or are given) meaning by them. This analysis can be generalized to the other social or cultural systems and traditions (like science and art) that structure experience through contexts which invoke aesthetic, ethical, factual, as well as religious modes of response.

While the notion of a 'spontaneous' religiosity locates the source of a sense of God within each person, the gods have also been found within social groups and their traditions. Those contrasting interpretations cannot be examined simply by asking people what they believe they are doing. Experimental procedures can, however, indirectly test what might be involved, since our reactions are socially shaped as for example when we use information from other people to guide our feelings. Schachter and Singer (1962), for example, gave injections of either adrenalin or an inactive substance before their subjects were asked to join a group of either sad or happy people. It was found that those who had been emotionally aroused by the adrenalin reacted to the sad (or the happy) emotional climate of the group they were in, in a way that was consistent with it. Social control of this kind could be more common in religion than it is usually assumed to be.

In a similar way, people are influenced by the traditions and explanations they have accepted and the particular religious (or other groups) they belong to. Indeed, most people are influenced by those groups more than they can hope to change them. This may be one explanation for the evident success of enthusiastic forms of religion among those who disapproved of them initially, and were later swept into their contagious excitement. Other explanations of that 'social facilitation' are in terms of a dissonance theory, where the inconsistency between what is presented and a well-established position is itself a precursor to changes in attitude.

We must distinguish the ways people come to be influenced by a religion from what sustains them within it. While most of the evidence about those processes is retrospective, differences between the social backgrounds of religious people and the accounts they give of what has influenced them are too broad for us to find simple explanations there. (There were similarly great differences among the twelve Apostles, and in the interpretations of the life of Jesus, as Schweitzer showed in 1910.) The personal traits or types that have most often been aligned with religious characteristics depend on denomination (contrasting those in Catholic and Protestant traditions), movements or parties within those traditions (including the fundamentalism or liberalism that has been so easily aligned with closed- or open-mindedness), and the orientations to religious belief itself, especially, as we have seen, in Gordon Allport's distinction between an extrinsic and the intrinsic or committed forms of religiousness. Other terms that have been used refer to committed and consensual, primary and derived, or authoritarian and humanistic forms of religion. But there is little evidence that those orientations have systematic links with other psychological traits, and either pole may have similar effects on the sense of well-being of those who find it plausible.

While a religion can be used for self-gratification or wish-fulfilment, to broaden one's interests or gain social recognition, most criticism of it has been directed to the immaturity or self-indulgence that is often either expected or detected there. Religious people who recognize the many ways there are to be 'religious' will approve of those that are most similar to their own preferences even if they may not be clearly articulated. To assess the impact of all the possible forms religion can take requires a detached stance and unbiased judgements about the relative value of each, not in terms of their truth or falsity but in other terms: Is the adherence devout or nominal? Is religion oriented to the law or to prophecy, to sacrifices or steadfast love? Is it in an individual, institutional or 'religionless' form?

Religious argument

Some of the scales used to measure religion were briefly examined in Chapter Three. A largely unresolved problem concerns their validity, and whether they can consistently assess what they purport to measure, whether that is the content of religious beliefs, orientations to belief, religion's success in resolving predominantly social or personal problems, or how the beliefs are protected (perhaps dogmatically). Believers confront the same dilemmas when they assess their own or others' beliefs. While the Church draws on the wisdom of a range of exemplary figures to illustrate every stance that can be identified, the decision-rules that individuals use to assess the credibility of what they are offered as a 'religion' have not yet been studied, beyond assuming that they have been thought up, involve a wager about life after death, or that some people will believe whatever they are told. The force of such social influences are harder to measure than are the effects of physical events. It is now clear, however, that we readily go beyond the information we are given to reach conclusions about what is likely to happen. These intuitive inferential strategies have recently been identified by Nisbet and Ross (1980), and by Kahneman, Slovic and Tversky (1982), who have shown that we over-generalize our prior knowledge, beliefs or experience, neglecting formal logic and the rules of probabilistic inference. Our common reasoning is therefore intuitive rather than scientific, not because we cannot avoid drawing false conclusions but because we misread the continued availability of events already in our experience and memory and have a bias to accept prior theories and hypotheses. This bias means that we identify religion with psychological factors and self-serving needs, rather than with socialization and teaching about our traditional culture and customs.

Nisbet and Ross (1980, p. 30) emphasize that there 'has been surprisingly little research on those beliefs and theories shared by the mass of people in our culture'. Most of the work that has been done has examined individual differences among believers, following up the lay theories of behaviour which assume that we are driven by internal, enduring and consistent dispositions that override the demands of particular situations. Despite that, socio-demographic findings show that, for example, those from the middle classes are over-represented among churchgoers, which suggests that religions appeal to, or select their supporters from, those who share particular social characteristics.

The recognition of these effects has produced a recent 'paradigm' shift in the psychology of religion towards the view that any religion is enacted by individuals against well-defined social processes: the interaction of personal and social factors is therefore crucial in every analysis of religion. This view insists that beliefs shape our interpretations of experience, especially when they support actions that are socially recognized or approved. The consistency of behaviour across situations that any dispositional view of religion would expect has not been found, and religious actions can only be predicted for quite precise intentions, like proposing to go to church on a particular occasion, because our church-going is constrained by broader social rules and conventions. This could be one reason why religion operates as a schematic or organizing principle among those who support a particular tradition. Religion does not have the same boundaries or defining characteristics for every group. The 'scripts' that specify what religious people should do in particular contexts, for example at the Sunday morning service in a particular church, must be expected to vary across groups, places and time. Abstract scripts that refer to temptation or sin are also important, since they make events (or accounts of them) comprehensible and predictable, but not in the same way for every group. 'Scripts' can also explain why stock 'characters' or roles can completely consume clergy, lay readers, sidesmen, or members of a congregation, on appropriate occasions. Yet we must not disregard the problems of those who occupy these roles as they 'contextualize' their own actions.

Contrasts between spontaneity and order or between metaphorical and literal meanings have been able to clarify what people say about themselves, but they do not take account of the deliberate control we have over what to reveal to strangers, what to say in a religious conversation, or how to act in a church. Self-report questionnaires rather than direct observations have been the most widely used method of gathering those data, despite their vulnerability to religious and secular prescriptions about the proper answers to any question. For example, what children might say about religion to other children is likely to be quite different from what they will say to a parent,

Sunday-school teacher or stranger since they are taught to be sensitive to what it is appropriate to ask or disclose. Furthermore, very few people derogate religious beliefs directly. Partly because of this, the positive correlations that are consistently found between separate measures of religion might simply reflect the consistency and social approval given to religion by those who *know* what they are expected to say, since religious beliefs are brought into use when attention is focused on 'religious' goals. But those goals cannot be identified without reference to their context and its appropriate actions. Correlational studies therefore make religions appear more coherent than other areas of life, although insiders to religious issues and beliefs make well-differentiated responses to doctrines and their content, with contrasts between the fear and fascination in religion (following Rudolf Otto) and between debt and desire (as Antoine Vergote put it) as well as to more traditional interpretations of myths, symbols and religious realities.

Summary

We must look beyond what can be believed to the way the doctrines that support religious beliefs are justified or supported, and used by individuals and groups to *do* various things. William James (1985, pp. 491–2) wrote of a 'corporate commitment' to religion, and the Doctrine Commission of the Church of England in its report, *Believing in the Church* (1981), set a counterpoint between doctrines and personal belief. Social contexts that constrain self-presentation, what is allowed, and the experiences that can be claimed, readily overrule idiosyncratic demands for change, greater relevance, or religious innovation. Religion is, therefore, a predominantly conservative influence on social life.

The well-recognized ambiguity of religion as public *and* private, social *and* personal, secular *and* transcendental has made it a traditional field for psychological interpretations that must be empirically tested, although for too long we have disregarded commonsense interpretations. Systematic research will not necessarily threaten the Church's hold on its own domain. Although Blaise Pascal asserted in 1670 that there are two foundations of religion, 'one inward, and the other outward', popular theories of religion still contrast positive and negative evaluations of what is defined socially or personally as transcendental (involving 'mystery', 'miracles' and 'God as being') or tangible (like church institutions, authority, and even 'going to church'). But whoever will be religious must carefully follow the agreed rules for their religion, unless they would risk being identified as mad or fanatical.

11 Applying the Psychology of Religion to Religious Contexts

Beware of false prophets, who come to you in sheep's clothing, but inwardly they are ravening wolves.
Ye shall know them by their fruits . . .

Matthew 7.15–16

The psychology of religion applies what we know of general and social psychology to understanding the beliefs, behaviour and experience of those who are 'religious' or who find themselves in religious contexts. This is either done directly or by comparing them with those who are not religious. Although there are problems in deciding what 'religiousness' involves there appear to be fewer differences between those who are and those who are not religious than is commonly assumed. Despite that, some contexts and social roles *are* unequivocally 'religious', especially when they involve a church and its clergy and those linked with them whose work is sanctioned by a church.

While that is not an ideal way to specify what religion is, those who base their life in a religion (and for us that usually means Christianity) are by definition religiously engaged. The stereotypes of such people reflect cultural expectations about churches and other community settings, as well as the intentions of those who are involved there, with their conflicts over how to satisfy religious or secular demands. While that has been the subject of innumerable sermons, *individuals* can be expected to have differing attitudes or orientations to the religious doctrines and beliefs they are offered (or that they can find). Many people also expect religion to influence and be influenced by the secular context within which it is cast. Only within an enclosed community (or in a sect) is religion set well apart from other social or cultural processes. When those secular influences work in their favour, religious people are pleased with their 'relevance'; when they do not, they tailor their presentations to reduce the conflict, or retreat into their own preoccupations. Inconsistencies between religious and secular perspectives are resolved categorically by those who think closed-mindedly, while others find there is always more to learn or discover. Although they may accept Christian assumptions, they know there are other ways to realize a religious perspective.

Newton Malony (1978) collected autobiographical statements from eighteen Christian psychologists who answered the question, 'What is the difference that being a Christian makes in the life of a psychologist?' He answered the question for himself by saying that *any* vocation involves an expression of faith. Those who resist an organized religion might agree with Bonhoeffer's apparently paradoxical conclusion that we need a 'religionless Christianity', stripped of its institutional forms. Others who reject either a behavioural psychology *or* conservative Christianity might look only at the psychological states and motives that underlie our overt behaviour. Behaviourists too easily neglected those mental processes when they found them inconvenient in their attempts to develop a scientific psychology.

Although most people now know something about psychology, applying it is like applying religion. There is a variety of perspectives and one must be cautious before offering firm conclusions. But psychological methods, data, results and theories or interpretations do have a place in the study of religion, not least because they impinge on areas that have been traditionally dealt with by the Church, including the 'cure of souls', which is increasingly being taken away from the Church by mental health professionals, who usually concede only a minor place to their chaplains, leaving education as a continuing activity for the churches.

Scientific psychology

Society has looked to psychology for 'scientific' information and answers to basic questions about human nature, sexuality, aggression, morality, and how to organize social (and parish) life, expecting that objective data and well-constructed theories would deepen our understanding. While commonsense is often devalued by the experts' judgements, there might not be much in the psychology of religion that is counter-intuitive. But the Church has often failed to minister to the emotional needs of its people because it relied too heavily on the Bible or on its own traditions, or on experts who would speak for it about social or personality processes, psychotherapy, and social phenomena, rather than about friendship, determinism, choice and responsibility, the mind–body problem, or the role of authority. The psychologists' conclusions sound challenging to some because they question the effectiveness of therapy, healing, or other forms of ministry with a pragmatic approach that tests basic assumptions and values against empirical evidence. Others find the scientific theories of religion two-dimensional, because of their emphasis either on psychological or sociological analyses.

Gordon Allport tried to resolve that problem by suggesting that there are both institutional and individual perspectives on any religion, which he later turned into the extrinsic and intrinsic orientations that distinguish those who *use* their religion from those who would *serve* it. Spilka rephrased those individual perspectives as the 'consensual' and the 'committed' forms of religion, to which Batson added a quest orientation that is characterized by a doubt and tentativeness which faces 'existential questions in all their complexity, while resisting clear-cut, pat answers' and asserts that we do not know the final truth. Other forms of that quest might look for identification with a group or tradition as an anchor, not because it can satisfy individuals directly but because of the social relationships it gives them.

Understanding the varieties of religious experience and orientation, and of religious forms, is a fundamental problem that confronts any applications of psychology to religion. This is made more difficult by our uncertainty about the 'correct' stance. Should we persuade others to our views, or is our role primarily to serve them? In either case it is essential to be able to find out how people make sense of their religion and live as believers in secular contexts that do not always accept religious points of view.

Experimental psychologists have contributed to our understanding of what is involved in sensation and perception, learning and motivation, and in cognitive and emotional responses. The study of personality differences and abnormal functioning, developmental and social psychology, and the use of procedures for data collection and statistical inference have also enabled us to evaluate the various forms of coping, and more recently to stress the need for assertiveness, 'personal growth', well-being, and happiness. While it is easier to study how a malfunctioning system works, psychologists have not entirely neglected what maturity involves, with their orientations that range from the materialist perspectives of behaviourism to an almost mystical transpersonalism.

Counselling and guidance

Psychologists can give expert advice on surveys that assess the level of support for organizational change, or about knowledge and beliefs or the problems and difficulties of parishioners. While fact-finding surveys are an obvious way to apply the expertise that has been developed in the social sciences to pastoral planning, any survey must be built from a sympathetic understanding of the issues and of the theoretical questions they involve. Psychologists can be as prejudiced as religious people in their design of a survey.

The prejudices of psychologists are especially important when questions about counselling and guidance are involved, since the theories that influence the practice of psychotherapy seldom rest on clear and unequivocal findings. In the broadest terms, therapy has roots in the religion and medicine that depended on faith healing and hypnotism. Both aimed to modify feelings and knowledge, especially about the self, and attitudes and behaviour that proved to be troublesome. Success depended on the extent to which it was possible to ameliorate the harshness of life.

Therapy now aims to teach new skills and change beliefs about the causes of personal discomfort and dissatisfaction or helps to develop more adaptive convictions about one's self and the realities of life. The techniques that are used range from the non-directedness of a passive, reflecting therapist dealing with an active client, to a collaboration in which the clients are helped to change by an active therapist who 'knows' what it is best to do. Counselling to reduce the tension or resentment and lack of skill that builds up in a society carrying a residual Christian ethic relies more on explicit techniques of behavioural control and relaxation. While all these approaches can aim to change specific behaviours, the social context, or attitudes to the self, there is now a clear trend towards eclectic methods because of dissatisfaction with any single procedure.

Counsellors need the skill to know when to refer someone to another expert, whether because of their lack of progress, their specific problems, or a mutual lack of sympathy. They also need to take special care with those whose problems focus on a specifically religious content, distinguishing a spiritual need or malaise from a true psychological pathology, and to identify those whose state puts them at variance with society or with some facet of it. Differential diagnoses are never easy, and it is better to be cautious than to expect the worst.

Therapy and counselling now involve a separate profession that has a broadly social focus on mental health to help cope with frustration. Whether God should be explicitly talked about in counselling depends on the solutions proposed and whether religion is thought appropriate for the empathic understanding that can achieve shared goals and experiences of 'unconditional positive regard'. Studies of the results of counselling have shown few effects that are attributable to differences in technique, since broad skills are needed to produce psychological changes. Yet Bergin (1983) argued that to define the goals for change with a clinical pragmatism that aims to reduce discomfort through a humanistic idealism neglects religion as 'the most important social force in the history of man'. To move the focus from individuals to transcendental values brings a value system to the fore that is often disguised by professionalism and a scientific perspective that could now be losing some of its authority as a source of objective truth.

Because many religious perspectives can be easily misunderstood and misused some conception of what 'mature' religious responses entail is essential. It has already been noted that this involves integrative attitudes to the self and to one's identity, acknowledging the need for personal development and self-actualization and accepting the values of autonomy, mastery and independence in one's orientation to social reality, to social relationships, and to the environment. Therapists as well as counsellors also need to have some knowledge of what disturbed behaviour implies and an understanding of the nature of learning, emotional reactivity, whatever lies outside awareness, and typical reactions to crisis. The value of modelling others to produce and maintain change, as well as the wide range of normal reactions must also be recognized. The fact that individuals, families, and social groups now ask for help through supportive, and non-directional, modes of treatment increases the forms of intervention that are possible.

It is within everyone's experience that in a marriage, as well as in more distant relationships, loneliness, failure and a lack of credibility require constant attention (except among those using denial as their defence). 'Pop' solutions to these problems are self-fulfilling panaceas that avoid theory and sound evidence, beyond a few supposedly typical but exemplary success stories that merely reflect the skill and appeal of the popularizers themselves as they attack 'negative thinking' or whatever else is disapproved. If these approaches involve psychological (or religious) perspectives that are derived directly from 'Freudian', 'Jungian' or other schools of thought, some help is needed to evaluate them and their results. A few argue that the psychology of religion ought to be about how to make those evaluations.

Commonsense

While a knowledge of psychology probably helps people cope with the problems in their own life, it should also encourage a tolerance of others' views in a way that gently questions their received solutions. Despite that, the way a problem is presented constrains the solutions that can be proposed, so that a sacramental confession imposes different demands from a request for counselling or from a casual encounter in a church, park, or High Street.

Facile interpretations of the reasons for action in terms of any set of 'motives' disregard the freedom we have to reconstruct or reframe untoward responses and events in the way we talk about them and appeal to experience, specific events, or another's advice. We all make mistakes, and need not assume that an ideal observer could identify the 'real' reasons for our actions. While early psychologies encouraged that kind of detective work, theories about the ways we use attributions to account for actions and their role in constructing a stable social and personal environment have forced a recognition of the equally valid yet different perspectives that actors and observers have on any action. Since the boundary between social and idiosyncratic responses favours what is socially accepted, religious concepts sanction and make sense of the world by appealing to shared beliefs and interpretative rules about the past and the future.

Religion is more readily available to some groups of people, but especially to women, young people and the very old, and, like other religious traditions, Christianity offers its own perspectives on personality development and functioning (through an increasing 'knowledge of God' and pastoral care). Yet the skills we now need to give help, advice or counsel, and to teach, may be overridden by those who insist that 'the Bible says . . .' Religiously conservative groups also draw their boundary between the religious and the secular more inclusively for religion, thereby controlling the advice they give. Skill-based models of how to counsel are a useful alternative to the interpretative theories that inevitably attract controversy.

Religious belonging is often fixed by a person's own criteria, despite rules about initiation and the other obligations that must be satisfied. It has been found therefore that self-reported religious practice is the most effective criterion of religiousness, not least because it is public and involves an explicit commitment of time. We are still not sure, however, what makes religious beliefs plausible except for their familiarity and evocative power.

This analysis leaves us with the conclusion that many arguments (as opposed to any evidence) about religion are built on theological, traditional, and social grounds. Questions about, for example, the proper age for confirmation are therefore referred to a tradition and not to the commitments that can be expected, and it is still widely assumed that the hope of a life after death allays anxiety.

But training is needed for anyone to know *how* to react to religion and its doctrines, just as we are trained (with varying degrees of efficiency) in music, mathematics, or gardening. In reacting to their training, some people will be alienated by particular religious perspectives, although we cannot yet predict who will be affected by them either positively or negatively. Any training or guidance must therefore be offered cautiously, respecting the integrity of others' perspectives and their ability to change as they learn, avoiding generalizations from our own conclusions. To recognize value-based judgements is an important step towards a decentred or scientific perspective on our own actions, and on those of other people.

The religious insights that preceded the current bio-psycho-social models of action, which recognize the essential unity of individuals and their social groups, were forgotten by the advocates of positivism and reductionism. Computer and information processing models have recently helped to overturn the mechanistic theories of action which psychologists of religion tried to counter in the 1920s and 1930s with their psycho-dynamic and psychoanalytic models which accounted for what we would avoid but neglected growth, self-realization and competence. Religious groups which support newer psychotherapies still prefer to be reactive than to initiate change, which makes them vulnerable to the secular pressures that are increasingly dominated by mechanical (and structural) models of the market forces and economic imperatives that are expected to control us.

Most psychological theories now recognize the freedom of choice. But because the decision rules (and heuristics) that we use to decide what we should do are usually sub-optimal, people continue to buy lottery tickets and put their money on the football pools, disregarding the low probability of success but hopeful that fortune will smile on them alone. While not especially prudent (or socially responsible), gambling does involve an active search, rather than the passive attitudes that were once thought typical of most actions.

Institutionalized 'religion'

Religions offer a map in the search for rewards and to avoid failure. That map may define goals that entail a resignation to God's will and a kind of helplessness, or an active participation in faith or in works. Concepts of guilt and sickness and a moralism thinly disguised by the notion of a 'healthy life-style' that reduces smoking, weight, and fat, all separate the good self from what is bad. This is like the contrasts between sacred and secular, revelation and reason, this world and the other, nature and grace, and even between what is individual or social. Such antitheses leave many uncertainties about whether a withdrawn or a secular life, innocence or experience is better.

Choice is intrinsic to contemporary social life. While counselling or therapy might help us find out how to be 'in the world', an eclectic perspective on that is not necessarily bound by jurisdictional disputes, but looks for authentic solutions, perhaps with 'implicit' faith in justice, health and order, affirmation and autonomy. Making any of those solutions too explicit involves the institutionalizing handicaps that Dietrich Bonhoeffer countered with a 'religionless Christianity'. I would similarly argue for a 'religionless psychology of religion' just as Thomas Oden (1967) advocated a 'religionless psychotherapy'. Oden said that although

> Protestant theology has borrowed much from modern psychology, it has nonetheless yearned to cling to some territory which would remain distinctly religious. Yet psychotherapy has become increasingly sure of itself, able to get along quite well without the so-called 'God' of religion (to be distinguished from the God known in Christian faith, the God who reveals himself in Jesus Christ). Both Catholics and Protestants, however, continue to view the secularizing development with frenzied alarm as defection from the truth (p. 216).

'Religion' does not have to be restricted to specific domains like death, or aimed to rescue mankind from unhappy desperation with a security and apparent contentment that can be as false as the readily identified malaise it counters. Bonhoeffer wrote that, 'we must move out again into the open air of intellectual discussion with the world, and risk shocking people if we are to cut any ice' (cf. Oden, 1967, p. 221).

Theology and counselling can be seen as separate functions of the Church, the first as theory and the other as practice. Psychology holds a similar tension between theory and practice (at a lower level) but (hopefully) with a less obvious dogmatism, because it is identified with 'science' and with values external to any study, but subject to negotiation. Good research can, however, systematically monitor values and practices, looking at the effects in differently structured religious groups or communities of the emotional and social pathologies that include loneliness, physical illness, anger and impulse control (especially among men), or the nurture and self-sacrifice that has been left to women.

Instead of fostering controlled research, many church groups continue to sponsor descriptive analyses of their apparently declining religious belief and practice. While those studies seem to show that religion has lost its superficial appeal, they are usually designed in a way that cannot show *why* this has occurred. We need more challenging data to question received theories and find what *really* sustains people. We could even find that the values and viewpoints we have been trying to explain or influence are not held seriously. Those in the comfortable role of expert use techniques that obscure their weaknesses, and assume a role of moral arbiter, that easily misses critical conflicts in the problems they set out to study.

Summary

It may be time for the psychology of religion to examine more carefully the spiritual and other values of pluralistic and secular societies, helping to expose the reticence we have had about sharing any traditional meanings we have appropriated. That approach might enlarge our knowledge of the functions that religion serves, beyond its use to sanction, soothe, support, and answer impossible questions in a way that seldom challenges the realities of social life. Until we know the religious questions that *are* to be asked, we can only 'hope' to have answered the right ones with explanations that are in some sense still 'stories'. Although science now gives the most preferred answers to life's questions, religious texts give explanations that may be no less valid in their own domain, even without systematic and controlled (rather than revealed) data to support them.

12 Conclusions

POZZO: (*peremptory*) Who is Godot? . . .
VLADIMIR: Oh, he's a . . . he's a kind of acquaintance.
ESTRAGON: Nothing of the kind, we hardly know him.
VLADIMIR: True . . . we don't know him very well . . . but all the
same . . .
ESTRAGON: Personally I wouldn't even know him if I saw him.

VLADIMIR: But you can't go barefoot!
ESTRAGON: Christ did.
VLADIMIR: Christ! What's Christ got to do with it?
You're not going to compare yourself to Christ!
ESTRAGON: All my life I've compared myself to him.

Samuel Beckett, *Waiting for Godot*

Most of the arguments I have covered can be reduced to a subtle
interplay between an individual psychology of religion (and of its
'faith') and a social psychology which recognizes that 'we are members
one of another' (Eph. 4.25). Many of the conclusions point directly to
the role of experience, judgement or enlightenment, but still look
optimistically for the obscure personality-based processes that others
expect us to show, neglecting the ways we directly influence and are
influenced by other people. Furthermore, a few major interpretations
have kept reappearing, especially in relation to a social or personal
emphasis on the consequences, purposes, and orientations in a
commitment to religion.

Early psychologists emphasized a religion of solitude, which
William James described as 'a discharging lesion like that of epilepsy',
and as a 'mystical or theological hypothesis' (1985, p. 192). This gave a
continuing focus for psychological interpretations of religion which
supported lay beliefs about the role of personality traits, needs or
characteristics as major determinants of the differences between
individuals which then cumulate to produce recognizable differences
between groups of people. These ready explanations of religion
account for natural and supernatural experiences, for the way projections of unresolved fantasies, especially about parental figures, are
used to form coalitions with a God who controls impulses, relieves our
faults and our guilt about sin, or reduces our fears about death. The
formal evidence about these processes that has been summarized by
Argyle and Beit-Hallahmi (1975) and by Spilka, Hood, and Gorsuch

(1985) is agreed by those psychologists to be unconvincing. A Christian perspective on whatever religion might involve is more direct, but typically offers individual salvation as itself an object or goal of life.

The consequences of religion

Psychological perspectives on religion must avoid the suggestion that religious people have just dreamed up their beliefs for themselves, since our religious beliefs and doctrines are shared. A personal religion therefore embellishes or rejects what has been made available: it does not have to be understood in a reductionist way. William James (1985, p. 23) emphasized, 'In the natural sciences it never occurs to anyone to try to refute opinions by showing up their neurotic constitution.' Instead of trying to explain religion by some prior psychological imbalance, we might look for its consequences, and for the 'fruits' of religion that can persuade or convince others.

These consequences include the acknowledged importance of religion: for example, 91 per cent of people over fifty in the United States claim that their religious faith is either very or fairly important in their lives. In 1960, 89 per cent of people aged between eighteen and twenty-four, compared with 72 per cent in 1980, had agreed that that was so, although in a more recent study 22 per cent said they were 'not religious' while 2 per cent said they were atheist. Religion is, at least in the United States, too widespread to be simply an adaptive mechanism. There is clear evidence that social involvements are easily increased by attaching oneself to a church and religious people also report greater marital satisfaction and stability, and are less likely to have used non-prescription drugs. Religion therefore appears to have a strongly supportive social role, and it has been found to contribute to rated life 'satisfaction', so that 'the behaviour of religious people differs from that of the non-religious when religious norms differ from those of their society' (Spilka, Hood and Gorsuch, 1985, p. 286).

While these broad findings warrant further detailed confirmation, it is clear that there is an important interaction between religious *norms*, especially about social issues, and the related behaviour of those who hold themselves to be in some sense subject to those norms. The inconsistencies there reflect the ways interpretations of these norms themselves depend on religious orientations, and the uses to which they can be put by individuals. Those complex relationships are well illustrated by the links between religious attachments and mental disorders, since a religious system, with its supernaturalism, can focus psycho-pathological tendencies. It can also keep people in touch with social reality and so reduce their abnormal responses; or it can simply become a haven or refuge. A religion can also be actively therapeutic, as it is for so many people whose lives are not threatened by break-down. All of these effects are complicated by personal or social factors beyond religion, but especially by the coping skills and social inadequacies that need more searching and coherent study than they have yet been given. Many approaches to these problems can still be criticized for their subjective emphasis and their neglect of the explicitly social *and* public basis of religion in culture and tradition. In those roles it structures lives, through the systems of meaning and ritual that validate changes from one social position or status to another. But no research-based or commonsense solutions are episte-mologically neutral and too many studies have implied that either disbelief, or less commonly belief, is the more 'normal'.

While many of the welfare functions of religious institutions may have been taken over by the state or other public agencies, that leaves traditions, texts, rituals and rules to define the contexts within which individuals and groups can carry and express their religion. We must therefore ask, not what could have caused religion or how it arose, but what can religion do and what can be achieved with it. We might also ask how religion is transmitted between generations and who avoids its influence.

The evidence is overwhelming that parents (and other significant adults) convey religion to their children in such a way that they either accept it as a part of reality, or are alienated and distanced from it. Those who lapse from religion typically do so as a reaction against their parents' influence, when they are so challenged by other activ-ities, peer pressures and systems of disbelief that to 'switch out' is easier than making minor changes to their religious orientation. These subtle changes in perspective have been neglected in favour of the 'big' questions about whether religion involves a unique, explicit and coherent phenomenon, or whether it is subjective and diffused (cf. Dittes, 1969, pp. 618f). The answer to both questions is 'Yes', but depends on the data gathered, the groups being studied, and how the data are analysed. (Technical questions about the item sampling and data analysis involved have not been referred to here, because they are discussed in my book, *The Psychology of Religious Belief* (Brown, 1987).)

Psychologists of religion have less often looked for evidence at the level of world religions than within Christianity, and usually within one or two denominations. In that sense, psychology itself and the psychology of religion have followed the readily defined issues, such as what characterizes religion and what is the impact of family and school on its transmission, and narrow questions about the effects of religion on individuals. Comparisons of religious beliefs with other ideological systems such as science, politics, art or literature, have been neglected. Assuming that choice is possible, an expressed confidence in religion, or in any other system, does not have to imply a coherent stance, and we do not yet know what makes particular religious or other beliefs seem plausible to everyone who accepts them.

Rules for religion

An awareness or experience of religion implies that knowledge about it is structured schematically. Just as we might have 'learned the rules' about riding on the underground in London and feel uncertain when first visiting New York about how the fares on the subway should be paid, so we know what to do in our own church, what some implications of the biblical stories are, what to say when we are asked how (and why) the world was created, and what religious people are like. We have also learnt when to appeal to religious sanctions, what it is appropriate to pray for and what effects can be expected through prayer.

'Frame', 'script', 'schema', and 'prototype' are the terms currently used to describe how such information is organized psychologically so that it can be recursively patterned into longer sequences, even covering the whole of life. It is also common for specific patterns or sequences like church services or committee meetings to be well structured. While those scripts emphasize contextual factors they also assume that those involved in them will be 'religiously motivated' (however that is construed) rather than primarily concerned with social prestige or personal gain. The deadly sins and the cardinal virtues, and the attributes of those who practise or resist them, are similarly schematic.

In defining the contexts and legitimate fields for religion we must recognize that other social changes have reduced its sphere of operation and allowed translations of religious concepts. So 'sin' has become 'sickness' or 'alienation', 'holiness' has become 'wholeness' and 'providence' 'trust'. It is not obvious whether these translations involve a further separation between sacred and secular, a growing abstention from religion, or simple substitutions of activities and descriptive terms. Instead of applying their religion to the social world, many people have moved it inside themselves, to be used for consolation, to deal with distressing events or to alleviate their depression.

Psychological theories are also used schematically as we try to understand other people and share conclusions with them. Confidence can be shattered by actual findings about what a majority says it believes or has decided to do. Furthermore, any talk about religion must recognize the social constraints on its traditional formulations. In that sense, analyses of religion could be strengthened by more explicit comparisons with work on science, politics or sport. The earlier comparisons with magical, psychotic, or animistic *thinking* neglected the social role of religion and it was not recognized that religion is both more and less than a leisure pursuit.

While religion and social science have often been in conflict because they touch similar topics, when people are asked how a knowledge of psychology or of the psychology of religion can be applied to religious problems and issues, those who would resist a systematic analysis of it argue that their own common sense (or their implicit psychology) is enough, since religion is a resource to be drawn on in crisis. Analyses of religion that have hoped to distinguish its 'good' or mature from the 'bad' or immature forms, or that would explain why people do not all have the same degree of commitment, imply an evaluation against at least some criterial or prototypical views.

The general question, 'Is religion good or bad?' is not easy to answer empirically. As with other evaluative research, we must first specify the possible forms of religion, the characteristics of those involved with it, the way they use religion in different contexts, and the effects they expect. With that approach we might identify those for whom religion is 'a-schematic', and not a part of their life or their self-concept.

The social variables that mark off religious people include age (younger and older), sex (female), education (poorer) and occupation (higher status). Any identifiable values or beliefs are confounded by what is implicitly prescribed there. Despite that, the relationships between psychological variables and religious commitment are curvilinear, whether they involve adherence to a church or a sect, to the Law or the Gospel, with extrinsic or intrinsic orientations on this world or the other, through belief or practice. This means that the high and low scorers on those religious variables tend to be more similar to one another psychologically and socially than they are to those who are neutral, or uncommitted to religion. These relationships are further confounded because conservative religious systems favour control through juridical and other explicit criteria that offer ready solutions to social and personal problems (particularly concerning sex). Religion only ceases to compete against other belief systems or activities among those who have developed settled beliefs, have never rebelled against it and innocently accept it, or among those for whom it is a self-fulfilling theory that filters the 'truth' about the world.

Psychology and religion

For many religious people, psychology is seen as more of a threat than a resource, despite their eagerness for *and* resistance to psychological analyses. To tailor a psychology of religion so that it deals only with the acquisition and protection of belief, and perhaps with its consequences, is not a good solution, since religion is most clearly articulated when it is being criticized and people rise to defend or identify with it. They are most likely to disclose their 'true' perspectives then, reiterating an orthodox position or revealing heterodox opinions about issues such as the ordination of women or the language of the liturgy.

Any defence they offer can become data for further analyses that translate what is expressed into psychological, social, sociological or anthropological terms. To look for another Newton, or for a Freud of the social sciences who will integrate those perspectives is like waiting for Godot. Psychologies of religion are of necessity based in processes that control personal judgements and social responses. While the early psychology of religion aimed to describe what it involved, and the meanings it encompassed or developed, the approaches now dominant examine how belief and action are embedded in altruism, in assumptions about a just world, conservatism, orthodoxy, obedience to authority, and in other aspects of personal and social life.

The 'facts' of religion are then found in the ways doctrines and rituals link with belonging, experience, meaning, and whatever consequences are actively sought or passively accepted. Nothing of that is quite solitary, since the most that can be achieved there is madness or a counter-revolutionary freedom confined to the self. Yet most religious groups continue to support an individualistic perspective. While investigators cannot escape their own religious knowledge or prejudices they are constrained by the conventions of social science that rely on western, and typically Christian, categories for their analyses. Phenomenologists of religion have therefore been more successful than psychologists in describing generically sacred experiences, because they are not so closely bound to the 'correct' data sets, and can use historical methods to document typical responses.

Religious phenomenologists have also shown that non-Christian traditions have their own explanations and descriptions, and that their theologies and practices are congruent with their own cultures, and not easily transported to another. Imagine, for example, Christian students finding Islamic students preparing for their prayers in the wash-room of an Australian college or university and asking them to stop or join a Bible study group. If each side tries to explain themselves to the other, the Muslims probably hope to be able to get on with what they are doing. The explanation of the dominant group is not necessarily correct, but a trans-cultural psychology of religion is still to be fully developed.

Psychological models of Christianity that have aligned the processes involved there with terms like causal judgement, social influence, expectancy, delayed gratification, altruism or hopefulness will not automatically translate or generalize to other religious traditions. Yet Christianity is a domain to which psychology has been traditionally applied, whether to describe it, make predictions about it, or interpret its symbols. From a religious perspective, psychological principles (which *have* changed) can be used to evaluate the acceptability of religious practices or doctrines, or to help develop the skills of those engaged in pastoral work.

While psychological skills can help to resolve the tension between independence and conformity, religion itself cultivates a sense of awe or fascination, it can soothe and support, answer difficult questions, challenge one to a just life, and foster binding obligations and self-fulfilment in solitude or in a community. All these solutions can draw on the sense of transcendence that William James contrasted against a moralistic pursuit of what ought to be. Religion does not have to be reduced to the ethical control that fascinated Durkheim, or to the infantile dependence Freud found in it, although there are negative forms of it to be set against a religion of 'healthy-mindedness' that is not disenchanted with ordinary life. Not every religious utterance is a cry for 'Help!' Yet as in the rest of psychology negative states can be most easily examined because they appear more focused than the wide range of adaptive responses.

Religion also involves difficult questions about who becomes a target for evangelism. Individual decisions, rather than any pressures to conform, are more obvious among those who have changed their religious affiliation than among those who have found that what they have been offered can be easily taken for granted. To contrast the internal states or conclusions that might make people 'religious' against their social background and the other external factors that predisposed them to accept religious beliefs and follow its practices might, however, prove less constructive than it would be to find how religion works and what it can do. Comparisons with language, art, and with whatever lies between reality, representations of reality, and the imagination could help to establish that.

Wittgenstein (1958) noted that a two-dimensional diagram of a

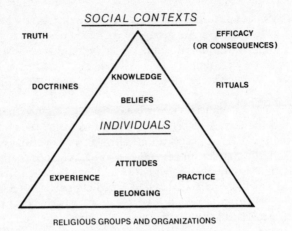

Fig. 6. *A psychological model for religion.*

triangle can be 'seen' (or interpreted) as a hole, a solid figure, a geometrical drawing of half a parallelogram, and as a picture of a mountain, wedge, arrow or pointer. But we cannot yet specify what we must know to be able to 'see' a diagram as a picture *or* as an abstract shape. In a similar way we cannot specify what produces a 'success-ful' socialization to become religious, any more than to become a musician, a mathematician or a scientist.

Not only is there always more to know, there is more than one way to find what we do not know. The exponents and carriers of religion know only some of the scripts their followers or would-be followers might accept, especially if they are to keep on the right side of the often fragile boundary between faith and unbelief. While there are as yet no computer simulations of religiousness, those simulations would have to include individual and social factors, belief, practice, experi-ence, and the influence of tradition. These influences are shown schematically in Figure 6.

Epilogue

It has been suggested that an empirical social science may be more useful in documenting historical changes than in identifying the facts and principles of social behaviour. While early sociologists relied on historical evidence to define the role of religion in society, the survey data that have been gathered over the last fifty years have become an important resource for contemporary historians and other interpreters of religion to show how the acceptance of religion has changed. Although psychologists have been more interested in the place and function of religion in the lives of individuals, they have not completely neglected the external or social influences that produce religious conservatism and orthodoxy from the institutional memberships and traditions that seem as necessary for those who are 'religious' as for those who would adapt to other aspects of society. A great deal of our research looks, therefore, as if it supports the existing roles religion provides and an expectation that individuals should fit themselves into the established traditions, defecting when they can no longer accept those norms.

But what can someone who is religiously uncommitted say about the adaptiveness of religion, granted their lack of involvement with the ways it might maximize happiness or foster a mature outlook and extend existing links between religion and society? Could useful advice about how to be 'religious' be derived from current psychological findings and principles? That depends! If one accepts that an external criterion defines what religion must be like, whether it is received or revealed, one will not change the approved expression of religion because of any psychological studies of religious people. If, however, one accepts that people construct religious meanings for themselves, those developed alignments and orientations can be tested against explicitly religious and psychological findings and principles. Psychology, unless it continues to regard itself simply as a descriptive or normative science, could acquire a role as midwife and critic.

There should be little conflict between religion and psychology when church attendance and membership, images of God and patterns of belief are being studied. But when those results are interpreted, conflicts can emerge if, for example, psychological principles are used to sanction a recommendation that people should change their beliefs, alter their religious practice, move to another 'stage' of religious growth or attack an opponent's views. These conflicts are most pronounced in discussions about religious maturity, the role of women in the churches, constraints on religious change, how to meet the demands of the unchurched, in theological and ecumenical questions, and in attitudes to newer traditions such as Pentecostalism and modern Catholicism. These issues are more than just a matter of stepping outside the role of psychologist into a more committed attitude. Godin's developmental tasks (see pp. 102–3 above) emphasize that few people have a developed sense of the historical context of the gospel, of Christ's role as a *sign* of God's action in the world, and of whether the gospel is more concerned with liberation than moralism. Perhaps these tasks are not important for those who keep their social relationships within a local church and who would be lost to it if that system failed to offer the support they need, if too many theological differences were aired, or if groups in the church challenged the leadership or the clergy.

On the other hand, those who are 'mature' can be expected to hold to a decentred view of reality that is not restricted by a particular tradition or denominational group, and to understate their own experience despite its evident authenticity. With such a perspective, religious education might aim to sharpen the separate dimensions of life and discourage purely utilitarian attitudes towards belief systems, replacing doubt with a trusting acceptance of both the dark and the light sides of existence.

When an abstract perspective is used to interpret the symbolism of the Eucharist and other sacraments, the meaning of biblical passages, specific doctrines, or the nature of the Church, the conclusions might range from accepting the necessity of institutional religion to rejecting it altogether in favour of a 'religionless' Christianity, or from an incorrigible pessimism about the human condition to a confidence and trust in human nature or the benevolence of the creator. To focus political perspectives on received religious forms, to clarify the hidden essence of those forms or simply to preserve them is similar to making a distinction between the surface and deep structures of language, either of which can be a legitimate focus for study.

While psychological analyses of religion can be used to support and justify existing religious patterns, they have more often been used to criticize and expose the failures. But social science's approach to religion has tended to be convergent and regressive, concentrating on what is now believed, rather than on what religion might be able to do, in a performative sense (following J. L. Austin's emphasis on what we can do with language). In fact, the psychological analogies between language and religion deserve more attention than they have received, since language is another complex system from which we make precise selections to solve particular problems.

The small amount of action-oriented research that has been published does not break out of the boundaries set by work that ranges from intensive studies of outstanding people to extensive studies of the attitudes and beliefs of large samples of well-defined populations, as in the European and the Australian Values Studies (Abrams et al., 1985; Bouma, 1987). These procedures are more often closed than open-ended, especially in their analyses of data, as if what we ought to know is already recognized and has only to be reached for. That attitude is certainly not the one that is expected of a religious orientation that is open-minded, decentred or abstract in its thinking and accepts the necessarily approximate or provisional nature of the accounts of our experience of the world.

Conclusion

Psychologists have exposed (and even specialized in) reductionistic answers to the question of why people believe in God. These answers have included social control, relief from distress, and compensation for inherent weakness. While some would argue that although religion *is* constructed, everything else that we know or experience is too (Arbib and Hesse, 1986). John Bowker (1987, p. 86) even asserts that the familiar placard should read, 'Prepared to meet thy God', to emphasize that the majority who belong to one or another religious camp have been, as it were, born there and subsequently make only minor adjustments to what they are given through the structures in which they were cast. Each of us has a reciprocity with our environment, our experience and understanding: psychology is as much a part of that process as is religion itself.

In a more detached way the methods of psychology have been used to describe religious beliefs and practice and to improve counselling and pastoral work by documenting the characteristic features of particular situations, and interpreting the results through concepts like orthodoxy, group cohesion, commitment, altered states of awareness and social support. Educational psychologists have shown that children often not only fail to understand what they are taught about religion, but develop their own explanations and constructions of it and their world. That realization helped to bring religious instruction closer into line with current educational practice, which was itself influenced by earlier psychological theories.

No data are collected from a passive memory store, since responses are always tailored for their context. A similar process of selection and self-presentation is involved as we accept or reject what any religion makes available, although it is not clear exactly *which* processes shape what those who know us well recognize to be *our* perspective on religion or on the world. Those perspectives may be acquiescent or involved, accepting or challenging established interests. An aggressive psychology (or religion) does not have to assume that researchers', clinicians', or theorists' knowledge has priority over that of their clients, who can hardly be expected to accept whatever they are told without answering back.

Gordon Allport (1955) deliberately called one of his books *Becoming* to stress the need for change and development. Later stages in personal development tend to be towards more critical views of received knowledge, and to the recognition that our reality is constructed and reconstructed, and not directly apprehended. We need not find a religious psychology resting on Christian insights and doctrines behind the pyschology that explains 'why', and less often 'how', religious individuals carry a religion. But we can expect insight into how we learn what to say about religion and how that knowledge is organized, and how to identify people as maturely (or immaturely) *human*, rather than just religious or irreligious. As a normal activity, religions offer, but can also impose, order and a lively structure on the stream of life. The forms of religion that become dominant depend on the orientation that is adopted to it.

References

Abrams, M., Gerard, D., and Timms, N., eds, (1985). *Values and Social Change in Britain*. London, Macmillan.

Allport, F. H. (1934). 'The J-curve hypothesis of conforming behavior.' *Journal of Social Psychology*, 5, 141–83.

Allport, G. W. (1950). *The Individual and his Religion: A Psychological Interpretation*. New York, Macmillan.

Allport, G. W. (1955). *Becoming: Basic Considerations for a Psychology of Personality*. Yale University Press.

Allport, G. W. (1966). 'The religious context of prejudice.' *Journal for the Scientific Study of Religion*, 5(3), 448–51.

Allport, G. W., Gillespie, J. M., and Young, J. (1948). 'The religion of the post-war college student.' *The Journal of Psychology*, 25, 3–33.

Arbib, M. A. and Hesse, M. B. (1986). *The Construction of Reality*. Cambridge University Press.

Argyle, M. (1958). *Religious Behaviour*. London, Routledge and Kegan Paul.

Argyle, M., and Beit-Hallahmi, B. (1975). *The Social Psychology of Religion*. London, Routledge and Kegan Paul.

Back, C. W., and Bourque, L. B. (1970). 'Can feelings be enumerated?' *Behavioral Science*, 15, 487–96.

Bassett, R. L. et al. (1981). 'The shepherd scale: separating the sheep from the goats.' *Journal of Psychology and Theology*, 9(4), 335–51.

Batson, C. D. (1976). 'Religion as prosocial: agent or double agent?' *Journal for the Scientific Study of Religion*, 15(1), 29–45.

Batson, C. D. and Ventis, W. L. (1982). *The Religious Experience: A Social Psychological Perspective*. New York, Oxford University Press.

Bell, R. M. (1985). *Holy Anorexia*. University of Chicago Press.

Bergin, A. E. (1983). 'Religiosity and mental health: a critical re-evaluation and meta-analysis.' *Professional Psychology*, 14(2), 170–84.

Bouma, G. D. (1987) *The Religious Factor in Australian Life*. Melbourne, World Vision.

Bowker, J. (1973). *The Sense of God: Sociological, Anthropological and Psychological Approaches to the Origin of the Sense of God*. Oxford, Clarendon Press.

Bowker, J. (1987). *Licensed Insanities: Religions and Belief in God in the Contemporary World*. London, Darton, Longman and Todd.

Brown, L. B. (1973). *Psychology and Religion: Selected Readings*. Harmondsworth, Penguin Books.

Brown, L. B. (1981). 'The religionism factor after 25 years.' *Journal of Social Psychology*, 107, 7–10.

Brown, L. B. (1985). *Advances in the Psychology of Religion*. Oxford, Pergamon Press.

Brown, L. B. (1987). *The Psychology of Religious Belief*. London, Academic Press.

Brown, L. B. and Forgas, J. P. (1980). 'The structure of religion: a multi-dimensional scaling of informal elements.' *Journal for the Scientific Study of Religion*, *19*(4), 423–31.

Caplovitz, D. and Sherrow, F. (1977). *The Religious Drop-outs: Apostasy among College Graduates*. Beverley Hills, Sage.

Capps, D., Rambo, L., and Ransohoff, P. (1976). *Psychology of Religion: A Guide to Information Sources*. Detroit, Gale Research.

Clark, W. H. (1958). *The Psychology of Religion: An Introduction to Religious Experience and Behavior*. New York, Macmillan.

Colby, A. and Kohlberg, L. (1987). *The Measurement of Moral Judgment: Volume 1. Theoretical Foundations and Research*. Cambridge University Press.

Crandall, V. C. and Gozali, J. (1969). 'The social desirability responses of children of four religious-cultural groups.' *Child Development*, *40*, 751–62.

Darley, J. and Batson, C. D. (1973). 'From Jerusalem to Jericho: a study of situational and dispositional variables in helping behavior.' *Journal of Personality and Social Psychology*, *27*(1), 100–8.

Deconchy, J. P. (1967). *Structure génétique de l'idée de Dieu chez des catholiques français*. Brussels, Lumen Vitae Press.

Deconchy, J. P. (1980). *Orthodoxie religieuse et sciences humaines, suivi de (Religious) Orthodoxy, Rationality and Scientific Knowledge*. Paris – Le Haye, Mouton.

Deconchy, J. P. (1985). 'Non-experimental and experimental methods in the psychology of religion.' In L. B. Brown, *Advances in the Psychology of Religion*, pp. 76–112. Oxford, Pergamon Press.

Deconchy, J. P. (1987). 'Les méthodes en psychologie de la religion: leur évolution récente.' *Archives de Sciences Sociales des Religions*, *63*(1), 31–83.

Dittes, J. E. (1969). 'Psychology of religion.' In G. Lindzey and E. Aronson, *The Handbook of Social Psychology*, 2nd edn vol. 5, pp. 602–59. Reading, Mass., Addison-Wesley.

Dittes, J. E. (1971). 'Two issues in measuring religion.' In M. P. Strommen, *Research on Religious Development: a Comprehensive Handbook*, pp. 78–108. New York, Hawthorn Books.

Doctrine Commission of the Church of England. (1981). *Believing in the Church: the Corporate Nature of Faith*. London, SPCK.

Doctrine Commission of the Church of England. (1987). *We Believe in God*. London, Church House Publishing.

Donahue, M. J. (1985). 'Intrinsic and extrinsic religiousness: the empirical research.' *Journal for the Scientific Study of Religion*, *24*(4), 418–23.

Durkheim, E. (1915). *The Elementary Forms of the Religious Life*. London, Allen and Unwin.

Dykstra, C. and Parks, S., eds, (1986). *Faith Development and Fowler*. Birmingham, Alabama, Religious Education Press.

Elkind, D. (1963). 'The child's conception of his religious denomination, III: The Protestant Child.' *Journal of Genetic Psychology*, *103*, 291–304.

Erikson, E. (1958). *Young Man Luther: A Study in Psychoanalysis and History*. New York, W. W. Norton.

Erikson, E. (1969). *Gandhi's Truth*. New York, W. W. Norton.

Erikson, E. (1974). *Dimensions of a New Identity*. New York, W. W. Norton.

Eysenck, H. J. (1954). *The Psychology of Politics*. London, Routledge and Kegan Paul.

Farberow, N. L. (1963). *Taboo Topics*. New York, Atherton.

Feather, N. T. (1964). 'Acceptance and rejection of arguments in relation to attitude strength, critical ability and intolerance of inconsistency.' *Journal of Abnormal and Social Psychology*, 69, 127–36.

Festinger, L., Riecken H., and Schachter, S. (1956). *When Prophecy Fails*. Minneapolis, University of Minnesota Press.

Fishbein, M., and Ajzen, I. (1974). *Belief, Attitude, Intention and Behaviour: An Introduction to Theory and Research*. Reading, Mass., Addison-Wesley.

Fowler, J. (1981). *Stages of Faith*. New York, Harper and Row.

Francis, L. (1985). 'Personality and religion: theory and measurement.' In L. B. Brown, ed., *Advances in the Psychology of Religion*, pp. 171–84. Oxford, Pergamon Press.

Francis, L., and Carter, M. (1980). 'Church-aided secondary schools, religious education as an examination subject and pupil attitudes to religion.' *British Journal of Educational Psychology*, 50, 297–300.

Frank, J. D. (1961). *Persuasion and Healing: A Comparative Study of Psychotherapy*. Baltimore, Johns Hopkins Press.

Freud, S. (1933/1971). *New Introductory Lectures* (ed. James Strachey), London, Allen and Unwin.

Freud, S. (1985a). *Civilization, Society and Religion*. The Pelican Freud Library, Vol. 12. Harmondsworth, Penguin Books.

Freud, S. (1985b). *The Origins of Religion*. The Pelican Freud Library, Vol. 13. Harmondsworth, Penguin Books.

Fromm, E. (1950). *Psychoanalysis and Religion*. New Haven, Yale University Press.

Fullerton, J. T. and Hunsberger, B. (1982). 'A unidimensional measure of Christian orthodoxy.' *Journal for the Scientific Study of Religion*, 21(4), 317–26.

Furnham, A. (1984). 'The protestant work ethic: a review of the literature.' *European Journal of Social Psychology*, 14, 87–104.

Galton, F. (1883). *Inquiries into Human Faculty and Development*. New York, Macmillan and Co.

Gilligan, C. (1982). *In a Different Voice: Psychological Theory and Women's Development*. Harvard University Press.

Glock, C. Y., and Stark, R. (1965). *Religion and Society in Tension*. Chicago, Rand McNally.

Glock, C. Y., Ringer, B. B., and Babbie, E. R. (1967). *To Comfort and to Challenge*. Berkeley, University of California Press.

Godin, A. (1964). 'Belonging to a church: what does it mean psychologically?' *Journal for the Scientific Study of Religion*, 3(2), 204–15.

Godin, A. (1971). 'Some developmental tasks in Christian education.' In

M. P. Strommen, ed., *Research on Religious Development: a Comprehensive Handbook*, pp. 109–54. New York, Hawthorn Books.

Goldman, R. (1964). *Religious Thinking from Childhood to Adolescence*. London, Routledge and Kegan Paul.

Gorsuch, R. L. (1968). 'The conceptualization of God as seen in adjective ratings.' *Journal for the Scientific Study of Religion*, 7, 56–64.

Gorsuch, R. L. (1984). 'Measurement: the boon and the bane of investigating religions.' *American Psychologist*, 39(3), 228–36.

Gorsuch, R. L., and Smith, C. S. (1972). 'Adolescent contraceptive behavior: a review.' *Psychological Bulletin*, 98(3), 538–68.

Gorsuch, R. L. and Spilka, B. (1987). 'The *Varieties* in historical and contemporary contexts.' *Contemporary Psychology*. (in press).

Greeley, A. M. (1974). *Ecstasy: A Way of Knowing*. Englewood Cliffs, Prentice Hall.

Greeley, A. M., McCready, W. C., and McCovat, K. (1976). *Catholic Schools in a Declining Church*. Kansas City, Sheed and Ward.

Harms, E. (1944). 'The development of religious experience in children.' *American Journal of Sociology*, 50, 112–22.

Harrel, S. (1977). 'Modes of belief in Chinese Folk religion.' *Journal for the Scientific Study of Religion*, 16(1), 55–65.

Hartshorne, H., and May, M. A. (1928). *Studies in Deceit*. New York, Macmillan.

Hay, D. (1982). *Exploring Inner Space: Scientists and Religious Experience*. Harmondsworth, Penguin Books.

Hood, R. W. (1976). 'Mystical experience as related to present and anticipated future church participation.' *Psychological Reports*, 39, 1127–36.

Hood, R. W. (1978). 'Anticipatory set and setting: stress incongruities as elicitors of implied experience in solitary nature situations.' *Journal for the Scientific Study of Religion*, 17, 278–87.

Hunsberger, B. and Brown, L. B. (1984). 'Religious socialisation, apostasy and the impact of family background.' *Journal for the Scientific Study of Religion*, 23(3), 239–51.

Jahoda, M. (1958). *Current Concepts in Positive Mental Health*. New York, Basic Books.

James, W. (1889). 'The psychology of belief.' *Mind*, 14, 321–52.

James, W. (1902/1985). *The Varieties of Religious Experience*. Harvard University Press.

Jung, C. G. (1958). *Psychology and Religion: West and East*. London, Routledge and Kegan Paul.

Kahneman, D., Slovic, P., and Tversky, A., eds, (1982). *Judgment under Uncertainty: Heuristics and Biases*. Cambridge University Press.

Kildahl, J. P. (1972). *The Psychology of Speaking in Tongues*. New York, Harper and Row.

King, M. B., and Hunt, R. A. (1975). 'Measuring the religious variable: national replication.' *Journal for the Scientific Study of Religion*, 14, 13–22.

King, N. (1986). *African Cosmos: An Introduction to Religion in Africa*. Belmont, Calif., Wadsworth.

Kohlberg, L. (1963). 'Moral development and identification.' In H. W. Stevenson, ed., *Yearbook of the National Society for the Study of Education*, pp. 277–332. University of Chicago Press.

Lawrence, P. J. (1965). 'Children's thinking about religion: a study of concrete operational thinking.' *Religious Education*, 60, 111–16.

Lenski, G. (1961). *The Religious Factor: A Sociological Study of Religion's Impact on Politics, Economics and Family Life*. Garden City, Doubleday.

Lerner, M. J. (1980). *The Belief in a Just World: A Fundamental Delusion*. New York, Plenum Press.

Leuba, J. H. (1896). 'Studies in the psychology of religious phenomena.' *American Journal of Psychology*, 7, 309–85.

Long, D., Elkind, D., and Spilka, B. (1967). 'The child's conception of prayer.' *Journal for the Scientific Study of Religion*, 6, 101–9.

Malinowski, B. (1925). 'Magic, Science and Religion.' In J. Needham, ed., *Science, Religion and Reality*, pp. 18–94. New York, Macmillan.

Malony, H. N., ed., (1978). *Psychology and Faith: The Christian Experience of Eighteen Psychologists*. Washington DC, University Press of America.

Malony, H. N., and Lovekin, A. A. (1985). *Glossolalia: Behavioral Science Perspectives on Speaking in Tongues*. New York, Oxford University Press.

Martin, J. and Westie, F. (1979). 'The tolerant personality.' *American Sociological Review*, 24, 521–528.

Miller, G. (1972). *Psychology: The Science of Mental Life*. Harmondsworth, Penguin Books.

Mol, J. J. (1985). *The Faith of Australians*. Sydney, Allen and Unwin.

Morrison, D. M. (1985). 'Adolescent contraceptive behavior: a review.' *Psychological Bulletin*, 98(3), 538–68.

Mosher, W. D. and Goldscheider, C. (1984). 'Contraceptive patterns of religious and racial groups in the United States, 1955–76: convergence and distinctiveness.' *Studies in Family Planning*, 15(3), 101–11.

Mulaik, S. (1964). 'Are personality factors raters' conceptual factors?' *Journal of Consulting Psychology*, 20, 506–11.

Munsey, B., ed., (1980). *Moral Development, Moral Education and Kohlberg*. Birmingham, Alabama, Religious Education Press.

Nisbet, R., and Ross, L. (1980). *Human Inference: Strategies and Short-comings of Social Judgments*. Englewood Cliffs, Prentice Hall.

Oden, T. C. (1967). *Contemporary Theology and Psychotherapy*. Philadelphia, Westminster Press.

Ostrom, T. M. (1969). 'The relationship between the affective, behavioural and cognitive components of attitude.' *Journal of Experimental Social Psychology*, 5, 12–30.

Otto, R. (1923). *The Idea of the Holy: An Inquiry into the Non-rational Factor in the Idea of the Divine and its Relation to the Rational*. (tr. J. W. Harvey). Oxford, Oxford University Press.

Pahnke, W. N. (1966). 'Drugs and mysticism.' *International Journal of Parapsychology*, 5(2), 295–324.

Piaget, J. (1933). 'Children's philosophies.' In C. A. Murchison, ed., *A Handbook of Child Psychology*. Clark University Press.

Polanyi, M. (1958). *Personal Knowledge: Towards a Post-critical Philosophy.* University of Chicago Press.

Popper, K. (1945). *The Open Society and its Enemies.* London, Routledge and Kegan Paul.

Pratt, J. B. (1920). *The Religious Consciousness.* New York, Macmillan.

Robinson, J. A. T. (1963). *Honest to God.* London, SCM Press.

Robinson, J. P., and Shaver, P. R. (1973). *Measures of Social Psychological Attitudes.* Ann Arbor, University of Michigan Survey Research Center.

Rokeach, M. (1960). *The Open and Closed Mind: Investigations into the Nature of Belief and Personality Systems.* New York, Basic Books.

Rokeach, M. (1973). *The Nature of Human Values.* New York, Freeman Press.

Sargant, W. (1957). *Battle for the Mind.* New York, Doubleday.

Schachter, S., and Singer, J. E. (1962). 'Cognitive, social and physiological determinants of emotional state.' *Psychological Review*, 69, 379–99.

Schneider, L., and Dornbusch, M. (1950). *Popular Religion: Inspirational Books in America.* University of Chicago Press.

Schweitzer, A. (1910/1948). *The Quest for the Historical Jesus.* New York, Macmillan.

Singer, M. T. (1979). 'Coming out of the cults.' *Psychology Today*, 12, 72–82.

Spilka, B., Hood, R., and Gorsuch, R. L. (1985). *The Psychology of Religion: An Empirical Approach.* Englewood Cliffs, Prentice Hall.

Spock, B. (1955). *Baby and Child Care.* London, Bodley Head.

Starbuck, E. D. (1899). *The Psychology of Religion: An Empirical Study of the Growth of Religious Consciousness.* New York, Scribners.

Stark, R. S. and Glock, C. Y. (1968). *American Piety and the Nature of Religious Commitment.* University of California Press.

Stringer, M., and Cairns E. (1983). 'Catholic and Protestant young people's ratings of stereotyped Protestant and Catholic Faces.' *British Journal of Social Psychology*, 22, 241–6.

Strommen, M. P., ed., (1971). *Research on Religious Development: A Comprehensive Handbook.* New York, Hawthorn Books.

Sundén, J. (1974). *Religion psykologi: problem och methoder.* Stockholm, Proprius. (And a symposium on 'Sundén's Role-Theory of Religion' in the *Journal for the Scientific Study of Religion 26* (3), 367–411.)

Thouless, R. H. (1923). *The Psychology of Religion.* Cambridge University Press.

Thouless, R. H. (1935). 'The tendency to certainty in religious belief.' *British Journal of Psychology*, 26, 16–31.

Thouless, R. H. (1971). *An Introduction to the Psychology of Religion.* Cambridge University Press.

Thouless, R. H., and Brown, L. B. (1964). 'Petitionary prayer: belief in its appropriateness and causal efficacy among adolescent girls.' *Lumen Vitae*, 3, 123–36.

Thurstone, L. L., and Chave, E. J. (1929). *The Measurement of Attitude.* University of Chicago Press.

Tillich, P. (1957). *The Protestant Era.* University of Chicago Press.

Tylor, E. B. (1877). *Primitive Culture: Researches into the Development of Mythology, Philosophy, Religion, Language, Art, and Custom*. New York, Holt.

Van de Kemp, H. and Malony, H. N. (1984). *Psychology and Theology in Western Thought, 1672–1965: A Historical and Annotated Bibliography*. Millwood, N J, Krauss International.

Vergote, A., and Tamayo, A. (1980). *Parental Figures and the Representation of God*. The Hague, Mouton.

Webster, D. H. (1984). 'James Fowler's theory of Faith Development.' *British Journal of Religious Education*, 7, 14–18.

West, M. A. (1987). *The Psychology of Meditation*. Oxford, Oxford University Press.

Westoff, C. F. (1979). 'The blending of Catholic reproductive behavior.' In R. Wuthnow, ed., *The Religious Dimension: New Directions in Quantitative Research*, pp. 231–40. New York, Academic Press.

Wicker, A. W. (1971). 'An examination of the "other variables" explanation of attitude behaviour inconsistency.' *Journal of Personality and Social Psychology*, 19, 18–30.

Wicker, A. W., and Mehler, A. (1971). 'Assimilation of new members in a large and a small church.' *Journal of Applied Psychology*, 55(2), 151–6.

Wiles, M. (1976). *What is Theology?* Oxford, Oxford University Press.

Wittgenstein, L. (1958). *Philosophical Investigations*. Oxford, Basil Blackwell.

Wittgenstein, L. (1970). *Lectures and Conversations on Aesthetics, Psychology and Religious Beliefs* (ed. Cyril Barrett). Oxford, Basil Blackwell.

Wright, D. (1971). *Moral Development: A Cognitive Approach*. Harmondsworth, Penguin Books.

Wuthnow, R. (1978). *Experimentation in American Religion*. Berkeley, University of California Press.

Yinger, J. M. (1977). 'A comparative study of the substructures of religion.' *Journal for the Scientific Study of Religion*, 16, 67–86.

Further Reading

Suggestions about what to read on the psychology of religion depend first on the grounding one has already and whether general or specific information is wanted. A more serious problem arises from the fact that source material for the psychology of religion is not held in many libraries, and even university bookshops usually stock only a few of the classics, although these books are helpful for those interested in knowing where current psychological studies of religion have come from. William James's *Varieties of Religious Experience* is usually available, and James E. Dittes (1973) has a good paper, called 'Beyond William James?' in C. Y. Glock and P. E. Hammond's *Beyond the Classics? Essays in the Scientific Study of Religion*, published in New York by Harper and Row (pp. 291–354). Sigmund Freud's work on religion is in Volumes 12 and 13 of the Pelican Freud Library published by Penguin Books, and some of Carl Jung's work on religion is in *Psychology and Western Religion*, published by the Princeton University Press in 1984. George A. Coe's (1916) *Psychology of Religion*, J. B. Pratt's (1907) *Psychology of Religious Belief* and J. A. Leuba's (1925) *Psychology of Religious Mysticism* have all been recently reissued in the United States.

General textbooks on the psychology of religion by Bernard Spilka, Ralph W. Hood and Richard L. Gorsuch (1985) and by Michael Argyle and Benjamin Beit-Hallahmi (1975) are soundly empirical, as are Mary J. Meadow and R. D. Kahoe's (1984) *Psychology of Religion: Religion in Individual Lives* and Raymond F. Paloutzian's (1983) *Invitation to the Psychology of Religion*.

My *Psychology of Religious Belief* (1987) concentrates on a single facet of religion, as does M. P. Strommen's (1971) edited collection of essays, *Research on Religious Development: A Comprehensive Handbook*, C. Daniel Batson and W. L. Ventis's (1982) *The Religious Experience: A Social Psychological Perspective* (New York, Oxford University Press), André Godin's (1985) *Psychological Dynamics of Religious Experience* (Birmingham, Alabama, Religious Education Press), and H. Newton Malony and A. A. Lovekin's (1985) *Glossolalia: Behavioral Science Perspectives on Speaking in Tongues* (New York, Oxford University Press).

If you are looking for psychological references to specific topics you could begin a search for them in Donald Capps, L. B. Rambo and P. Ransohoff's (1976) *Psychology of Religion: a Guide to Information Sources* and in Hendrike Van de Kemp's (1984) *Psychology and*

Theology in Western Thought, 1672–1965: A Historical and Annotated Bibliography, and in the *Psychological Abstracts* which come out each month and have annual and other indexes. These *Abstracts* cover what is published in academic serials or journals, including the *Journal for the Scientific Study of Religion*, the *Review of Religious Research*, and the *Journal of Psychology and Christianity*.

It is essential for a good grasp of the ways psychologists talk and write about religion to read technical papers, many of which are listed in the References. One ready source for recent assessments and reviews of several specific areas is *Advances in the Psychology of Religion*, edited by L. B. Brown (1985) and published by the Pergamon Press in Oxford. Robert Wuthnow (1979) edited a more sociologically oriented collection of essays on commitment, nominal religion, images of God, religion, delinquency, abortion and other topics, called *The Religious Dimension: New Directions in Quantitative Research* (New York, Academic Press).

Collections of papers from journals have been edited by W. A. Sadler (1970), Orlo Strunk (1971), Benjamin Beit-Hallahmi (1973), L. B. Brown (1973), H. Newton Malony (1977), John R. Tisdale (1980) and by J. Roland Fleck and John D. Carter (1981), but only the last two of these are still in print. The preference among sociologists to hold to their established theoretical positions is shown in Roland Robertson's (1969) collection of readings on the *Sociology of Religion* (published by Penguin) which *is* still in print.

There have been considerable theoretical changes in psychology recently, and it is essential to recognize the differences between developing a theory, setting out to test it, and using it to interpret or understand some phenomenon. Since religious processes and psychological theories exist independently of any psychology of religion, it is important to acknowledge the different interpretations of religion (including those discussed in John Bowker's (1973) book on *The Sense of God*) and the way psychology deals with psychological and social processes like memory, emotion, and social life itself. Alan Baddeley's (1983) *Your Memory: A User's Guide*, George Miller's (1966) *Psychology: The Science of Mental Life* and Roger Brown's (1986) *Social Psychology* are examples of good general introductions to these topics that are readily available.

Do not forget that it is important to find some help if you get stuck in looking for specific information. If you can't find other advice and would like to write to me at the School of Psychology, University of New South Wales, Kensington, NSW 2033, Australia, I will do what I can to help.

LAURENCE B. BROWN

Index of Names

Index of Subjects